THE PRAIRIE SCHOOL

Design Vision for the Midwest

THE ART INSTITUTE OF CHICAGO *Museum Studies*

THE ART INSTITUTE OF CHICAGO
Museum Studies

VOLUME 21, NO. 2

THE PRAIRIE SCHOOL

Design Vision for the Midwest

FOREWORD

New Forms, Old Functions: Social Aspects
of Prairie School Design

ROBERT TWOMBLY
Professor of History
The City College of New York

What makes the Prairie School comprehensible as an entity is less the prairie than the city, where "schools"—whether centers of intellectual inquiry or of artistic production—had for centuries been located. Without Chicago, and to a lesser extent other midwestern cities, there would have been no Prairie School and the term itself would have been an oxymoron. For the prairie was but the nearest tabula rasa upon which to inscribe urban objectives. The role of Prairie School participants was to domesticate the country for historically new middle and upper-middle classes. The Prairie School gave physical form to an urban sensibility, itself ancient, that in and around Chicago at the turn of the twentieth century was attracted to the avant-garde.

As Richard Guy Wilson points out in this issue, "the single-family suburban house" was "the heart of the Prairie School." For all the urban, commercial, and institutional work its members produced, and for all their furniture, stained glass, and other decorative arts of which Judith A. Barter writes in these pages, the Prairie School made its most profound impact beyond the city limits with detached dwellings for which those ornamental objects were by and large intended. Three publications that Mary Woolever discusses below confirm this point. Frank Lloyd Wright's 1911 Wasmuth portfolio (cat. no. 32), an overview of his career since 1893, contains seventy-two plates depicting fifty-four houses (including four service buildings), but only seventeen other structures. In his 1925 *Wendingen* anthology (cat. no. 33), which covers 1902 to 1922, twenty of the thirty-three buildings are dwellings. And three issues of *The*

Western Architect (published in 1913 and 1915) on Purcell and Elmslie (figs. 2–3), assembled as a book by the Prairie School Press in 1965 (cat. no. 44), had 108 illustrations, sixty-three of them houses or their furnishings. Janice Pregliasco's essay suggests, furthermore, that Marion Mahony Griffin and Walter Burley Griffin (figs. 4–5) adhered to this pattern during their "prairie" period, as calculations for other designers at that time—roughly 1900 to World War I—would probably demonstrate. One reason for *not* including Louis Sullivan (fig. 6) in the Prairie School, and instead thinking of him as a precursor, is not that he was part of an earlier generation (he was born in 1856, and therefore was no more than fifteen years older than most of the members of the Prairie School) but rather that he designed so few houses during the Prairie period.

Wright's career departed significantly from Sullivan's by introducing new possibilities for the social relations of their profession. Sullivan's career followed a familiar trajectory. Before the 1886–90 Chicago Auditorium Building made him and his partner Dankmar Adler famous, well over forty percent of their commissions were residential; after 1886, however, this figure dropped to only

FIGURE 1. Frank Lloyd Wright (1867–1959). *"Tree of Life" Window from the Darwin D. Martin House, Buffalo, New York,* 1904–06. Clear, opaque white, translucent aqua, and green glass in copper cames; 105.4 x 66.7 cm. The Art Institute of Chicago, Gift of the Antiquarian Society through the Mrs. Philip K. Wrigley Fund (1972.297).

eighteen percent. This was what most architects preferred, then and now: to pass up domestic work for larger, more remunerative projects. From 1900 through his last house in 1911, Sullivan designed seven dwellings, only two of which were constructed, whereas Wright erected at least eighty-two of a minimum 126 residential designs. The more telling figure, however, is that seventy-five percent of Wright's executed buildings during that period were dwellings, exactly as represented in the Wasmuth portfolio. Sullivan was unable and perhaps unwilling to take advantage of unprecedented growth in the middle and upper-middle classes or of their equally unprecedented departure from cities between the Civil War and World War I.

But that was Wright's great opportunity. He was the first architect in the United States to build an international reputation almost entirely on single-family residences. Even more important, however, he was the first to acquire fame without servicing the rich. His clients were "American men of business," the "upper middle third" of American society, as he liked to put it—the rapidly expanding, industrially based bourgeoisie. With Wright in the lead, the Prairie School developed a residential aesthetic suitable for this aspiring class. With Wright in the lead, the Prairie School—along with Irving Gill and the Greene brothers in California, and a few others—opened a new way for architects to be "visible," that is, to establish reputations beyond their immediate vicinities. That new way raised middle-rank bourgeois housing to the level of fine art.

It was apparent to those designers—and here is a minor dissent from Richard Guy Wilson's contention—that their buildings and household objects were not

intended for suburbanites, since what later became suburbs were at the time rural townships with expanses of farm and undeveloped land. Their art was intended, rather, for the "city man going to the country," as Wright himself put it in 1901, for the man seeking "a simple mode of living."[1] In other words, Prairie School architects specialized in the villa, which is, according to the eminent art historian James S. Ackerman, "a building in the country designed for its owner's enjoyment and relaxation." It "fills a need that never alters," that is "not material but psychological and ideological. . . . The villa cannot be understood apart from the city; it exists not to fulfill autonomous functions but to provide a counterbalance to urban values and accommodations." Its basic program "has remained unchanged for more than two thousand years since it was first fixed by the patricians of ancient Rome," but it "is typically the product of the artist's imagination and asserts its modernity."[2] Prairie School villas were new in form because they were built for a new and expanding class, but they were age-old in social program and in psychological function.

The work of the Prairie School aimed to make urbanites comfortable in the country by melding newly acquired city sophistication with nostalgia for rural values that was still very real to those suddenly successful businessmen and the efficiency-minded women who oversaw their households day to day. These urbanites may have been less sophisticated and country ambience less pacific than myth and belief allowed, and conventional architects may have pursued similar objectives, but the Prairie School successfully distinguished itself by buttressing old-fashioned social forms with avant-garde art forms. Although Prairie art and architecture may have been situated in

FIGURE 2. William Gray Purcell, c. 1915. Photo courtesy of the Northwest Architectural Archives, University of Minnesota Libraries, St. Paul.

FIGURE 3. George Grant Elmslie, c. 1936. Photo courtesy of the Northwest Architectural Archives, University of Minnesota Libraries, St. Paul.

FIGURE 4. Walter Burley Griffin.

FIGURE 5. Marion Mahony Griffin.

what had been, or was thought to have been, the prairie, its psychological and ideological impulses, in line with Ackerman's observations, were decidedly urban.

But not bohemian. As radical as Wright's dwellings may have appeared, he insisted that they were designed in "a cause conservative."[3] Wright asserted this in part to strengthen what today would be called "traditional family values": patriarchy and the submissiveness of women and children; solidarity among family members; retreat from threatening urban milieus; reunion with nature; respect for individual privacy; and spiritual renewal. This was accomplished with open-plan interiors encased within sturdy, noticeably protective yet amply fenestrated walls, which were given architectural expression with a clean, crisp, geometric, straight-edged aesthetic acknowledging the machinelike efficiency of the modern era. Newt Gingrich contends that computers will be the salvation of the poor. In the early twentieth century, some observers understood other new technologies to be salvation for the bourgeoisie.

In breaking new design ground, however, the Prairie School was hardly solipsistic. Richard Guy Wilson in his essay in this issue, and many others elsewhere, have examined the Prairie School's myriad sources of inspiration: the Arts and Crafts movement at home and abroad; the Stick and Shingle architectural styles; Japanese woodcuts; recent and contemporary art in France; the Queen Anne style in England; the bungalow fad; the Pure Form movement; the "Progressive" obsession with efficiency; "model home" demands of the modern "housekeeper"; and more. The scholar James F. O'Gorman has demonstrated the importance of H. H. Richardson's work, including his suburban railroad stations, for the Prairie aesthetic.[4] There is more to be said about those stations, however, particularly their resolution of opposites—urban modernity with rural traditionalisms—that spoke directly to the Prairie School. For in this genre, at

FIGURE 6. Louis H. Sullivan, c. 1895.

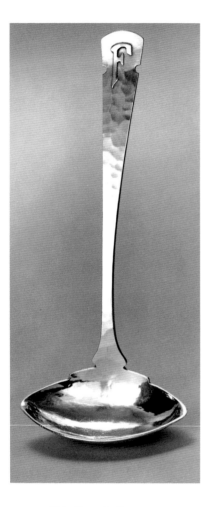

FIGURE 7. Kalo Shop. *Ladle*, 1905–14. Silver; 22.2 x 9.4 cm. The Art Institute of Chicago, Gift of Mrs. Sylvia S. Sights (1973.739).

least, Richardson also catered to the "city man going to the country."

Henry Hobson Richardson is widely considered the most important American architect of the nineteenth century. He was born in Louisiana in 1838, and moved to Brookline, Massachusetts, in 1874, and although much of his work was in the Boston area, he produced major buildings in Chicago, Pittsburgh, and Cincinnati. Richardson designed thirteen railroad stations between 1881 and his death in 1886, nine of them for rural or suburban settings.[5] They were erected for commuters and can be considered a new architectural type. At least seven of the nine have a "two-sidedness": contradictory images reconciled by the traveler's departure and return. Approaching from the village side, the commuter passed through a landscaped park—more often than not, by Richardson's frequent collaborator, Frederick Law Olmsted—that carried the leafiness of his own garden and of the town itself to the station door. Shrub-lined circular or winding carriage- and walkways might pass under a welcoming porte cochere that was sometimes the extension of a gently sloping, sheltering hipped roof. Rose bushes and vines framed the building's openings. A fireplace chimney capped the picturesque view. From the village side, the station reminded the traveler of home.

But on the platform side, domestic imagery gave way to technological, as soft forms became harder, making the station a two-directional zone of transition. Trees, shrubs, graveled paths, and inviting entryways were replaced by sharper edges, diminished leafiness, and a businesslike ticket window. The embracing cottage roof either became a clipped-eaved gable or was stretched longitudinally into an extended canopy, with its platform echoing the unrelenting straight steel rails, and with its supporting posts evoking the line of telegraph poles aimed at the city. A leisurely walk through the park thus culminated in emblems of modernity. In the evening, the sequence was reversed, of course. Rather than preparing the commuter for the fast-paced city, the station ushered him back to the peaceful countryside. By blending references to speed and machinery with those of bucolic domesticity, Richardson's commuter stations foreshadowed the Prairie School's union of urban sophistication and old-fashioned values.

The Prairie School did not appeal to those who, in their own minds, best represented sophisticated Chicago. That plutocracy, living on Prairie Avenue or on North Lake Shore Drive, preferred—like *arrivistes* before, since, and in other places—to surround itself with architectural styles and the kinds of art objects associated with prior aristocracies in order to elevate its social and cultural standing to a level commensurate with its economic and political power. Prairie School clients, by contrast, were likely to be smaller-scale manufacturers, merchants, and real-estate promoters, along with a sprinkling of professionals, who differed from the elite in one important respect: their hands-on experience overseeing every aspect of their businesses without delegating authority. They too were upwardly mobile, first-generation "self-made" men, but they were not much interested in fashion or being cultural arbiters, and they were still less concerned with living in the "best" neighborhoods, joining the "right" clubs, or immersing themselves in that network—was it even then dubbed "old-boy"?—of social, civic, and business organizations through which the elite perpetuated itself and ran the city. Prairie School clients were politically and socially conservative, to be sure, and comfortably heeled, but first and foremost they were "practical." They wanted their home lives to "work" with the same "no-nonsense" efficiency of their enterprises, without elaborate trappings; all of this meant that when they selected residential art and architecture they were not driven to emulate the florid tastes of a Harold F. McCormick or a Potter Palmer. For guidelines in these matters, they preferred to rely on their own "common sense."[6]

So here is one basis of the Prairie School's appeal. Its architecture and household objects tended toward simplicity of form with minimal embellishment. And the little embellishment there was made practical sense, highlighting a defining correlation between form and purpose. Robert R. Jarvie's candlesticks (cat. no. 23), for example, have broad, wafer-thin circular stands obviating tippage; slim shafts tapered like candles but with a hint of buttressing for stability; and rounded, up-curving cups with thin flanges that not only catch drips but, as smaller versions of their stands, also unify the composition. Clara Barck Welles's Kalo Shop soup ladle (fig. 7), ornamented only with the owner's initial, joins handle to bowl in an Art Nouveau gesture emphasizing the strength of the bond. Toward its top, where the stem broadens for firm gripping, there are two tiny notches; the broadening corresponds to the flare, and the notches to the shape, of the oval bowl—itself slightly pointed at either end for left- or right-handed pouring. These details give the ladle perfect horizontal and vertical balance. The candlesticks and ladle are simply and gracefully beautiful. Their ornamentation is essentially restricted to their own forms, the texture of worked silver, and the light the silver reflects. They also *look* practical, exactly as they should, given their purpose. There is virtually nothing superfluous about them.

When Prairie School objects were intended more for decoration than utility, they headed toward abstraction, regularly employing stylized floral patterns, linear geometries, architectonic qualities, and interlocking or balancing planes. Leaded windows like the one formerly attributed to George W. Maher (cat. no. 14) appeared again and again in Prairie houses: a stylized circular element is the only nonlinear insertion into an otherwise

FIGURE 8. Alfonso and Margaret Iannelli, c. 1915. Photo by the *Chicago Daily News,* courtesy of the Chicago Historical Society (DN-065600).

severely rectilinear composition representing a poppy plant. Marion Mahony Griffin's 1907 window (see p. 166, fig. 2) almost eliminated stylized representation with a matrix of upright and inverted V's, shaded and given perspective to approximate three-dimensional foliage. The precision-sawn finials with geometric inlays and tiny, shelflike projections on George Elmslie's 1912 standing clock (cat. no. 20) would have been at home as sculpture on Wright's 1913–14 Midway Gardens; the clock case's setbacks recall more than one Sullivan skyscraper proposal, and the front and side linear ornamentation resembles that of numerous Prairie house wall panels. Alfonso Iannelli's study of a sprite's head for Midway Gardens (cat. no. 13; see also fig. 8 in this essay) explores the possibilities of combining normally uncompanionable planes in a way often found in Prairie School chairs, in which independently articulated seats, backs, and arms slide past yet support each other, anticipating Gerrit Rietveld's more fully developed *Red-Blue Chair* of 1918 (see p. 129, fig. 10). Abstraction—masking but not always abolishing representation—was one artistic response to industrial technology that characterized but did not dominate Prairie School work.

As the reference to Rietveld and the de Stijl movement suggests, the Prairie School was not sui generis. Art Nouveau across Europe, the German and Austrian Secessionists, C. F. A. Voysey in England, Charles Rennie Mackintosh in Scotland, and H. P. Berlage in The Netherlands were but a few of the movements and individuals producing designs akin to those illustrated here. It is less instructive to "prove" who if any among them influenced whom than it is to note that new materials, manufacturing and installation processes, building types, and social classes generated by nineteenth-century industrialization stimulated an international revolution in art and architectural production. Designers in Europe and North America, convinced that a new machine age with its own zeitgeist had dawned, wrestled to develop art appropriate for it.

The Prairie School was part of this artistic confrontation with industralism. Eventually, the results came to be called "modernism"—an imprecise label that channeled others "isms," not to mention distinct individual, regional, and national differences, into a homogenizing stream—and it maintained momentum well into the post-World War II era. The claim has too often been made that the Prairie School and its commercially-based "Chicago School" predecessors were the architectural originators of modernism. This assertion, which is possible to sustain only if the rest of the world is ignored, proves completely groundless when the full range of Prairie School work is examined, as this issue permits. Similarities among utilitarian and decorative objects—

attempts to reconcile organic with technological motifs, for example—coupled with the social location of clients and customers here and abroad, work against the notion of American exceptionalism. What is suggested instead is that *some* members of the emerging industrial bourgeoisie, regardless of where they lived, were drawn to modern design as a way of asserting independence from industrial plutocracy.

Most bourgeois had little taste for this, preferring to purchase smaller versions of the houses and inexpensive interpretations of the objects gracing elite enclaves. Machine production and regional, even national, marketing facilitated mimicry, as did a level of affluence that enabled some to purchase the once exclusively patrician villa. Why some but not others of the rising middle classes headed toward modernity might be explained by examining psychologies, emotions, and personal preferences. But then, if individual motivation cannot be determined, collective tendencies can. More telling than any single acquisition is what the Prairie School as a whole offered the bourgeoisie.

Its work combined a taste of machine-age zeitgeist with the reassuringly, usefully familiar. Torn between the new and the old, wanting to procure the one but keep the other, its adherents marched resolutely forward while looking over their shoulders. The Prairie School was appealing because its level of abstraction never completely eliminated the literal or the representational: Marion Mahony Griffin's V-shaped elements were still recognizably plants, after all, while Frank Lloyd Wright's daring cantilevers were primarily intended to regulate the elements. Yet, at the same time, the designs were new, partaking of the avant-garde, and purchasers of Prairie houses or soup ladles could proclaim their informed, independent judgment.

In concert with European contemporaries, the Prairie School entered the new age enthusiastically, never quite leaving the old. Its artists and their public were a kind of bridge linking traditional to modern. But of fundamental importance is that for perhaps the first time in history the bridge over which fine—even avant-garde—art entered society was initially traversed by the middle class, not by the elite, making the Prairie School's social function every bit as important as its innovative forms.

FIGURE 9. Marion Mahony Griffin (1871-1962). *Shop Bungalow Plan, Elevation, and Perspective Section for the World Fellowship Center, near Conway, New Hampshire,* 1942. Delineated by Lola Lloyd. Ink on paper; 73.8 x 54.4 cm. The Art Institute of Chicago, Gift of Marion Mahony Griffin through Eric Nicholls (1988.8.1).

SHOPS

BUNGALOW

LIVING ROOM   KITCHEN
DINING ROOM
BEDROOM 2
BEDROOM 1   BEDROOM 3

SHOP 1

SHOP 2   SHOP 3

ENTRY

SHOP BUNGALOW PLAN
SCALE

COURT

PRAIRIE SCHOOL WORKS
IN THE DEPARTMENT OF ARCHITECTURE AT
THE ART INSTITUTE OF CHICAGO

RICHARD GUY WILSON
Commonwealth Professor of Architectural History
University of Virginia

Among the varying efforts to create an indigenous American art, the group known as the Prairie School stands out as one of the most original. Located in the Midwest, and hence more removed from the "contamination" of foreign precedent, as well as the preoccupation of East Coast architects with the colonial past, the members of the Prairie School liked to claim that they drew their sustenance from their native soil. Frank Lloyd Wright described his work in 1903 as "thoroughly saturated with the spirit of the prairie,"[1] and in many of his designs, as well as those of others, one can see abstractions of both the broad, flat landscape and the vegetation of the region.

In spite of the claim of a midwestern originality, the individuals who made up the Prairie School—architects, furniture and interior designers, craftsmen, painters, sculptors, and landscape architects—owed a complicated debt to both earlier American and foreign precedents. At home the quest for an unique American art had a variety of roots, though perhaps the earlier transcendentalists such as Ralph Waldo Emerson and the poet Walt Whitman laid the most immediate ground for the midwesterners. A very different precedent lay with the work of the 1870s and 1880s by eastern architects such as McKim, Mead and White (who by the 1890s and 1900s had shifted their allegiance to classicism) and Henry Hobson Richardson, who experimented with wood-shingled forms and houses with open interior halls. Buildings such as Frank Lloyd Wright's own house of 1889 in Oak Park, Illinois, or the earlier work of George Washington Maher, or even later designs such as Purcell and Elmslie's Bradley Bungalow of 1913 in Woods Hole, Massachusetts, indicate not just a debt to eastern architects, but a merging of sensibilities. The shingled architecture of the East Coast had drawn upon early American colonial buildings and also contemporary English and French preoccupations with wooden vernacular houses. Although most of the Prairie School architects rejected the "Beaux-Arts" as a stylistic preoccupation in their work, the French system of rational planning, the concept of a strong center to the plan, and the relation of space to building volume or mass still affected most of the midwestern architects. Another important influence was that of Japan and East Asia. Wright, for example, collected Japanese prints and visited there in 1905.[2] Many of the other architects and designers incorporated elements that recalled East Asian roots, from the upturned end of roofs to plain interior trim.

A more direct inspiration for the Prairie School, of course, lay with the international Arts and Crafts movement, which was concerned with design reform and the relation of production to social conditions. Founded by William Morris in England, the Arts and Crafts movement formed the basis for the continental Art Nouveau and the Vienna Secessionists, and it made a considerable impact

FACING PAGE, LEFT TOP: Louis H. Sullivan, 1885.

FACING PAGE, RIGHT TOP: Parker Noble Berry.

FACING PAGE, RIGHT BOTTOM: Francis Barry Byrne. Photo courtesy of the Chicago Historical Society (ICHi-25649).

FACING PAGE, LEFT BOTTOM: George Mann Niedecken (1878–1945). *Self-Portrait*, c. 1900. Photograph (probably silver print). Prairie Archives, Milwaukee Art Museum, Gift of Mr. Dean T. Niedecken.

across the United States, with many affiliated societies springing up. Morris and his designs were well known in Chicago, and several of his followers such as Walter Crane and C. R. Ashbee made frequent visits to the city and became friendly with architects like Wright. The Chicago Arts and Crafts Society, founded in October 1897 at Jane Addams's Hull House, included Prairie School designers such as Wright, Robert C. Spencer, Jr., Dwight H. Perkins, Myron Hunt, and Irving K. and Allen B. Pond, among others. These architects in turn had ties with another similarly Arts and Crafts-oriented organization, the Chicago Architectural Club. Founded in 1895, the club listed as members Howard Van Doren Shaw, George Niedecken, Elmer Grey, Arthur Heun, Richard Schmidt, Hugh M. G. Garden, and Louis Sullivan. The two groups frequently exhibited together at The Art Institute of Chicago. Indicative of the American shift toward the Arts and Crafts movement is Wright's essay "The Art and Craft of the Machine," in which he declared, "All artists love and honor William Morris." Wright, however, then claimed, "The Machine is Intellect mastering the drudgery of earth that the plastic art may live." Wright argued that the machine, instead of being the enemy, freed the craftsman and also allowed the repetition of simple shapes, the "very process of elimination for which Morris pleaded."[3]

To speak of the Prairie School as just architecture misses the important aspect—especially with regard to the Arts and Crafts movement—of its involvement with all the arts and its concern for social issues. The Prairie School building was conceived of as a total work of art: the interior decor, chairs, tables, windows, china, and the exterior landscape were important complements to the building's form. This high degree of participation by the designer implied a type of control in which non-Prairie School elements looked out of place and had to be relegated to back rooms or disposed of altogether. Some architects such as Wright even went as far as to design dresses and scarves for their clients.

Although the ideology of the Prairie School claimed a kinship with the freedom of the open prairie, few if any Prairie School buildings were ever built there. Some Prairie School buildings—projects for banks, schools, and other institutions—were located in cities or small towns, but the heart of the Prairie School lay in the new suburban settlements occurring around Chicago. In its emphasis upon the single-family suburban house, the Prairie School participated in a substantial revolution taking place as the middle class—aided by new methods of transportation such as the commuter railroad and the automobile—increasingly left the city for the safety and harmony of the suburb. Thus the relationship of the typical Prairie School house to the prairie itself lay more in an abstraction of nature, either the vines and blossoms of

Sullivan's ornament, or the more rectilinear geometry of Wright. Only a few architects actually tried to project a prairie community. Wright's examples from these years are fitful and incomplete, though he later returned to the subject with his Broadacre City scheme in the 1930s. A more substantial attempt is the work of Walter Burley Griffin and Marion Mahony Griffin—in particular, their design for a suburban enclave at Mason City, Iowa (see cat. no. 10).

That both Sullivan and Wright, with their very different aesthetics, could be included under the Prairie School banner indicates that this was not a movement about style as much as a movement about an ideology of independence. While the appearance of buildings and objects was of course crucial to the Prairie School, the movement went far beyond any narrow stylistic mannerism of ornament or form. Wright and Sullivan existed as only two poles of the Prairie School; beyond them there was the more independent work of Maher, Pond and Pond, and others, whose designs looked very different. What might be seen as an underlying formal or aesthetic link was, in fact, an attitude that conceived of broad, simple forms interspersed with concentrations of detail: in other words, a latitude of development that allowed for an independence of stylistic expression.

Lest there be any confusion, however, the term Prairie School is a relatively recent invention. Critics and writers at the time used a variety of labels for the group such as "Secessionist," "progressive," "protestants," "Chicago School," the "New School of the Middle West," "a Style of the Western Plains," or simply "Western."[4] Although the word "prairie" and identification with it existed at the turn of the century, Wright himself first used the term "prairie school" in an essay of 1935.[5] Not until the early 1960s did the term gain wide acceptance, and even then it indicated not a school so much as a group of like-minded individuals interested in creating an original American art.[6]

The golden years of the Prairie School lay between the late 1890s and World War I. Although Wright became disaffected with the group after 1909 and tried to claim that it reached its peak during his involvement, in truth some of the Prairie School's greatest successes came in the years just prior to the American entry into the war and in places beyond the Chicago suburbs such as Mason City, Grinnell, Cedar Rapids, and Sioux City, Iowa, or Red Wing, Minnesota, and LaCrosse, Wisconsin.[7] In small towns across the Midwest, and at times in other places such as Florida, Virginia, Washington, California, and even Puerto Rico, buildings with Prairie School elements appeared. With World War I and especially the aftermath of the Roaring Twenties, the Prairie School, according to many historians, ceased to exist.[8] Different occurrences caused the dispersal of the designers: Wright

CAT. NO. 1. Louis H. Sullivan (1856–1924)
Plant Form Studies, pl. 124, c. 1875
Copied from *Flore ornementale* (1866)
by Victor Marie Charles Ruprich-Robert
Pencil on tracing paper; 26.8 x 20.2 cm
Gift of George Grant Elmslie, 1988.44.8

floundered in problems of his own making; Parker Noble Berry, one of the most talented of the younger generation, fell to the influenza epidemic of 1918; Sullivan died an alcoholic old man in 1924; the Griffins moved to Australia; and Purcell retired. And some of the designers changed: Tallmadge and Watson, and William E. Drummond, for example, adopted the style of the Colonial Revival. But in actuality many of the architects, such as George Grant Elmslie, Barry Byrne, William Steele, and others, continued to design with Prairie School principles in mind. And overseas in Australia, where the Griffins worked, and abroad in Europe through publications and the visits of architects and designers, aspects of the Prairie School played a role in the development of modernism. Then in the 1930s, as already indicated, Wright returned to center stage with works such as Broadacre City. Other designers emerged to carry on the ideals.[9]

In the end, what we call the Prairie School today was not a unified movement but a particular coming together, first in the Chicago area and then expanding to the broader Midwest and beyond, of a group of individuals concerned with creating a new art form. The major vehicle for their endeavor lay with architecture, the traditional "mother of the arts," but all the other arts from furnishings to landscape and painting and sculpture played a role. The identity that the designers sought lay within the region, within the uniqueness of that changing landscape that makes up the American Midwest. And it is within those confines that they created an art that is both local and universal—one that changed how American art would be viewed.

1. Louis H. Sullivan, *Plant Form Studies*, pl. 124, c. 1875

At some point in the mid-1870s, possibly while he was working for Frank Furness in Philadelphia, or during his student years in Paris at the Ecole des Beaux-Arts, or perhaps in Chicago with William Le Baron Jenney prior to or after France, Louis Sullivan (1856–1924) executed a series of copies of plates from *Flore ornementale* by Victor Marie Charles Ruprich-Robert (1820–1887). Ruprich-Robert taught composition and design at the Ecole Imperiale et Speciale de Dessin in Paris. The studies he published between 1866 and 1876, of which this is one, are the foundations for Sullivan's later ornament and also illustrate one of the international sources of the Prairie School. Such copies were standard fare for the young architecture student of the time. Ruprich-Robert disliked most contemporary ornament, and he argued instead that the basis for a new ornamental language lay "in the flowers that we callously tread under foot." Claiming that man had a "genius" to either "simplify, or amplify, in a word modify,"[10] Ruprich-Robert pointed to both the inorganic, such as crystals, and then especially the organic, to the geometry of stems, buds, or seeds, and to the cylinders, triangles, quadrangles, pentagons, and other forms that could be found in all living things.

Certainly, Sullivan did not rely solely on Ruprich-Robert, and evidence exists that he studied Owen Jones's *The Grammar of Ornament* (1856) and Christopher Dresser's *Studies in Design* (1873–76), as well as *Gray's School and Field Book of Botany* (1857) by Asa Gray, but the Frenchman's lessons would remain with him for his entire life. Sullivan's copies of *Flore ornementale* are related to interior ornamental schemes that Sullivan worked on while in Paris, which he may have incorporated into his work for the Sinai Temple or the Moody Tabernacle, both of which were in Chicago but are now demolished. Elements of these copies show up in Sullivan's ornament for the Max M. Rothschild Store (1880–81; now demolished; fragments are in the Art Institute's collection), and the Jeweler's Building at 15–19 South Wabash, and they would form a basis for his later ornamental works.[11]

2. Adler and Sullivan, *Section of a Stencil from the Trading Room of the Chicago Stock Exchange Building*, 1893–94

This fragment of the decoration applied to the main trusses of the Trading Room of the Chicago Stock Exchange illustrates both the diverse nature of the origins of the Prairie School and the rich coloration of Sullivan's ornament. The actual building itself, erected in 1893–94, lay hardly within the Prairie School idiom of low-slung buildings that relate to the midwestern landscape. Designed by Sullivan with his partner Dankmar Adler (1844–1900), the Stock Exchange was a large commercial structure thirteen stories in height. But it was a brilliant demonstration of Sullivan's developing ornamental system, encrusted with terracotta on the exterior and, on the interior, cast and wrought iron, bronze, plaster, and painted decorations. The high point was the Trading Room, a double-height space located on the second floor. The interior measured thirty feet high, with the floor area sixty-four by eighty-one feet and a sixteen-foot-deep gallery running along one wall. The dominant feature of the room was the rich stenciling pattern that covered the upper portion of the walls and the various surfaces of the ceiling and its trusses.[12]

Stenciling had been a part of Sullivan's vocabulary since the 1870s, when he received commissions for some of his earliest Chicago interiors such as the Sinai Temple

FIGURE 1. Adler and Sullivan, Trading Room of the Chicago Stock Exchange Building, 1893–94. Reconstructed and reinstalled at The Art Institute of Chicago in 1977.

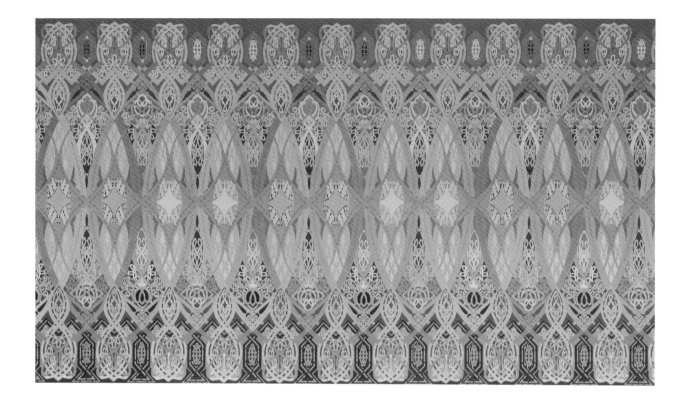

and the Moody Tabernacle. He developed his style further in decorating the Auditorium Building (1886–90) and the Schiller Theatre (1890–92; now demolished). The actual stenciling in the Trading Room was carried out by the firm of Healy and Millet; Louis J. Millet had been in Paris at the same time as Sullivan and came to Chicago in 1879 to set up a firm that specialized in decorative design and installation. He also taught at the School of the Art Institute. The stenciling was done on canvas that was then attached to the wall. Fifty-two different colors were applied to the section shown here. The scheme shows a growth and gradation from dark russet through yellows to a green at the top. The overall pattern is aligned vertically with a series of oval forms and different scales, and features intertwining stems and vines. The basic geometric organization was inspired by the various books by Ruprich-Robert and others that Sullivan had read earlier. There is a nervous energy to the scheme that also recalls Celtic decoration and Sullivan's Irish background.

After a lengthy battle over its preservation, the Chicago Stock Exchange Building was demolished in 1971, and portions of it were donated to institutions or sold. The Art Institute took on the task of preserving the former Trading Room, and installed it in its new east wing in 1977. The building's two-story entrance arch was reerected in the Art Institute's garden at Monroe Street and Columbus Drive.

CAT. NO. 2. Adler and Sullivan
Section of a Stencil from the Trading Room of the Chicago Stock Exchange Building, 1893–94
Executed by Healy and Millet
Oil on canvas mounted on panel;
143.7 x 305.4 x 1 cm
Gift of Mr. and Mrs. Arthur Dubin, 1971.747

3. Louis H. Sullivan, *Teller's Wicket from the National Farmers Bank, Owatonna, Minnesota,* 1906–08

Louis Sullivan's essentially decorative approach to architecture and his attempt to reconcile two opposing systems is wonderfully apparent in this bank teller's wicket. The overall form of the copper-plated cast-iron wicket and the opening into which it would be placed were emphatically rectilinear; the opening at bottom for transactions is a geometrically pure half circle. Sullivan and his draftsman, George Grant Elmslie (1871–1952), composed the ornamental opening around an interrupted vertical central axis, divided by several horizontal stretcher bars. But this geometry is subsumed under a florescence of plantlike growth, intertwining seed pods, clusters of berries, foliage, branches, and long tendril stems that climb upward on either side of the elongated

CAT. NO. 3. Louis H. Sullivan
Teller's Wicket from the National Farmers Bank, Owatonna, Minnesota, 1906–08
Copper-plated cast iron; 104 x 58 x 1 cm
Gift of the Winslow Brothers Company, 1908.73

oval of the opening. Two large and two small shield shapes immediately above the opening help focus the forms back to the central axis.

The cast-iron teller's wicket, manufactured by Winslow Brothers of Chicago, was part of Sullivan's elaborate decorative scheme for the National Farmers Bank in Owatonna, Minnesota.[13] The commission marks the beginning of Sullivan's late career, a period in which most of his work was outside Chicago and frequently for small-town banks. His designs for these institutions stood at odds with the prevailing norm of classicism. Sullivan had proclaimed his views about an indigenous American architecture in numerous writings, and the owner of the Owatonna bank, Carl K. Bennett, had read one of Sullivan's pieces and contacted him. The identity of the actual designer of many of the bank's details and, indeed, of its overall form has always been a matter of some controversy, since with one minor exception all of the drawings for this project are by Elmslie. Yet, although Elmslie is certainly responsible for carrying out the design, the conception belongs indisputably to Sullivan.

4. Louis H. Sullivan, "Manipulation of the Organic," 1922, pl. 2 of *A System of Architectural Ornament*

Sullivan's last great ornamental design and in a sense the summary of his beliefs was the short book *A System of Architectural Ornament According with a Philosophy of Man's Powers.* Composed and drawn in 1922–23 (just prior to his death in 1924), while he was also writing *The Autobiography of an Idea,* the *System of Architectural Ornament* was partly commissioned by the Burnham Library of Architecture at the Art Institute. It was created at the encouragement of several members of the Cliff Dwellers Club of Chicago and Charles Harris Whitaker, the editor of the *Journal of the American Institute of Architects,* under whose auspices both works were initially published.[14] The book is composed of a brief "Prelude" with an essay, "The Inorganic and the Organic," and twenty plates. Conceived of as an integral whole, the book is a meditation upon the underlying spiritual power of all things, the so-called "Germ," or as it is called in the plate shown here, "the Seed Germ." Both literally and metaphorically the Germ is the "seat of power," as Sullivan announced in his Prelude: "The seat of power and the will to love constitute the simple working idea upon which all that follows is based—as to efflorescence." According to Sullivan, the plates are arranged as a journey to spiritual awareness, and they contrast the inorganic—or that "which is lifeless, or appears to be so; as stone, the metals, and seasoned wood, clay, or the like"—with the organic. As he explains, "Nothing is really inorganic to the creative will of man." The plate shown here in a sense presents a summary of his thought and development; it is a vivid representation of the "morphology" of forms and the liberation of underlying energy.

The drawing itself is a technical accomplishment, not simply as it records the process of development, but also in its graphic technique. Sullivan used several different pencils both in hardness and in points to achieve his effects. He created a contrast between solid and shaded lines; some of the contours are only barely visible, while others stand out. Stippling and scumbling of the pencil over the texture of the rag board produced other almost ethereal effects. Finally, indicative of Sullivan's lifelong literary interests, nearly all of the drawings are inscribed with text; this one bears a reference to *Gray's School and Field Book of Botany*, which Sullivan had discovered back in the 1860s.

5. Irving K. Pond of Pond and Pond, *Perspective Rendering of a House in LaSalle, Illinois*, c. 1901

With its half-timbering, steeply pitched roof, and high form, this house by Irving K. and Allen B. Pond bears little resemblance to the normative Prairie School houses erected during the same time period by other midwestern architects. In actuality, however, English-based designs such as this one were far more common than one might imagine, and they were produced by many of the architects associated with the Prairie School. Examples include Frank Lloyd Wright's Nathan G. Moore House of 1895 in Oak Park, and numerous houses by Robert C. Spencer, Jr. Other architects more loosely connected with the Prairie movement such as Howard Van Doren Shaw, Arthur Heun, and Elmer Grey also frequently turned to English sources. Their work serves to indicate the strong presence of the English Arts and Crafts movement in Chicago and reveals the influence of two of the principal proponents of the English movement, C. R. Ashbee and

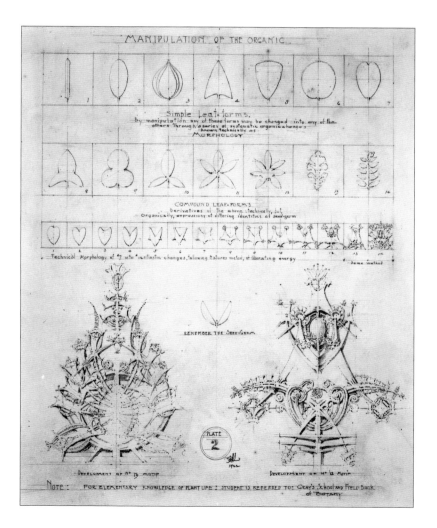

CAT. NO. 4. Louis H. Sullivan
"Manipulation of the Organic," 1922, pl. 2
of *A System of Architectural Ornament
According with a Philosophy of Man's
Powers* (New York, 1924)
Graphite on Strathmore board;
57.7 x 73.5 cm
Commissioned by The Art Institute of
Chicago, 1988.15.2

Walter Crane, who lectured in Chicago on several occasions between 1891 and 1908.

The architects Irving K. Pond (1857–1939), who was the main designer, and his brother Allen B. Pond (1858–1929) embodied much of the social conscience of the Prairie School.[15] Their work revolved around institutions, schools, auditoriums, and Jane Addams's Hull House, for which they designed numerous buildings. It was at Hull House that the Chicago Arts and Crafts Society was formed; both of the Ponds were members. In the late 1890s they had offices in well-known Steinway Hall on East Van Buren Street, along with Wright, Walter Burley Griffin, Dwight H. Perkins, Hugh M. G. Garden, and others.[16] In their designs the Ponds developed an abstracted historicism, typified by an extensive use of brick. Allen Pond devoted much of his activity to social causes, and he was the secretary of Hull House from 1895 to his death. Irving Pond wrote extensively on architecture, and although he initially displayed sympathies with Wright and his followers, by the late 1910s he had distanced himself considerably from the Prairie School.[17]

6. Vernon S. Watson, *Elevations and Sections of the Vernon Watson House, Oak Park, Illinois,* 1904

Vernon S. Watson (1878-1950) designed this house for himself at 143 Fair Oaks Avenue in Oak Park around 1904, shortly before he entered into partnership with Thomas E. Tallmadge (1876–1940) in 1905. Watson had attended Chicago's Armour Institute of Technology and Tallmadge had trained at the Massachusetts Institute of Technology. Their partnership lasted many years and they became known for a series of churches in the Chicago area. Their later work, especially after 1920, was in the Gothic and Colonial Revival idioms, but their earlier designs lay in the Prairie School line. An article in *The Western Architect* in 1915 called their work "progressive" and claimed that the partners endeavored to bring about "an evolution in architectural form . . . imbuing it with a real and genuine expression of our nationality."[18] Watson acted as the firm's chief designer, although Tallmadge became the better known because of his writing and teaching. In an article in 1908, Tallmadge first coined the term "Chicago School" to describe the work of the city's innovators in commercial design;[19] and later, in spite of his own reversion to revivalism, he defended Louis Sullivan's aesthetic revolution and insistence on originality in his popular history *The Story of Architecture in America* (1927). In the early history of the Prairie School, Tallmadge and Watson gained a reputation as house designers, and several of their works were published in Hermann Valentin von Holst's *Modern American Homes* (1912; see the article by Mary Woolever in this issue, pp. 142–43.).[20]

Watson's own house exemplifies a type of small house design, the so-called "four-square" that became an ideogram of the Prairie School. The origins of this essentially boxy and rectilinear form lie in middle-class houses

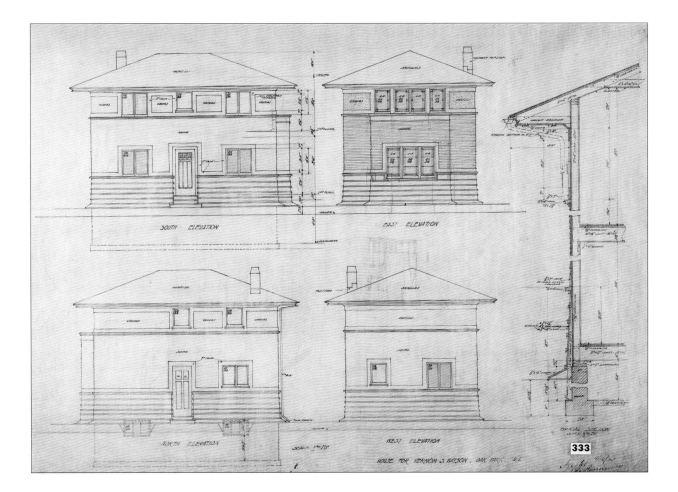

ABOVE: CAT. NO. 6. Vernon S. Watson
(1878–1950)
*Elevations and Sections of the Vernon
Watson House, Oak Park, Illinois*, 1904
Ink on linen; 46 x 66.7 cm
Gift of the estate of Vernon Watson,
1990.12.2

RIGHT: CAT. NO. 7. George Mann
Niedecken (1878–1945)
*Perspective Rendering of the Interior of the
Bresler Art Gallery, Milwaukee*, c. 1904
Ink on linen; 48 x 74 cm
Restricted gift of the Thomas J. and Mary
E. Eyerman Foundation, 1984.1297

FACING PAGE: CAT. NO. 5. Irving K. Pond
(1857–1939) of Pond and Pond
*Perspective Rendering of a House in
LaSalle, Illinois*, c. 1901
Graphite and watercolor on paper
mounted to board; 13.5 x 23.8 cm
Gift of the estate of Irving K. Pond, 1989.39

illustrated almost continuously in house pattern books from the mid-1800s onward. Frequently cubical or square in both plan and mass, the "four-square" was the standard housing stock used—and repeated ad infinitum—across the United States. The best known of the Prairie School variations was Frank Lloyd Wright's "Fireproof House for $5,000," published in the *Ladies Home Journal* in April 1907. Most of the Prairie School architects—Griffin, Purcell and Elmslie, John S. Van Bergen, William E. Drummond, and others—created variations on the type. In this case, Watson imparted a horizontal emphasis to the form with the low hipped roof, the high clapboarded basement, the heavy stringcourses, and the banking of the windows on the south and east elevations. The entrance is on center, and the rectilinear character is emphasized through trim and broad flat surfaces.

7. George Mann Niedecken, *Perspective Rendering of the Interior of the Bresler Art Gallery, Milwaukee,* c. 1904

George Mann Niedecken (1878–1945) ran an interior design firm in Milwaukee and frequently supplied furniture and designs for the Prairie School architects. His involvement varied from making furniture according to the specifications of other designers or architects to acting as a full collaborator in designing all interior elements. Those he worked with included Hermann von Holst, Marion Mahony, Dwight H. Perkins, Purcell and Elmslie, Spencer and Powers, Louis Sullivan, and Frank Lloyd Wright. He collaborated with Wright on twelve different commissions including the Dana, Coonley, and Robie houses, several of Wright's most important projects.

Niedecken was born in Milwaukee and attended art school there and also at The Art Institute of Chicago,

where he studied decorative design under Louis J. Millet.[21] He also attended school in England, traveling there and on the continent, where he gained first-hand knowledge of the latest decorative art movements emanating from Berlin, Paris, Turin, and Vienna. Around 1904 Niedecken worked intermittently at Wright's Oak Park studio, and in 1907 he established the Niedecken-Walbridge Company in Milwaukee. He always maintained close contacts with Chicago, exhibiting regularly in Chicago Architectural Club shows at the Art Institute. Although Niedecken produced many designs related to the Prairie architects, he also worked in other modes such as the Gothic Revival, the Colonial Revival, and various styles that might be called Art Nouveau or Secessionist.

This design for F. H. Bresler's Art Gallery in Milwaukee exemplifies Niedecken's proclivities for advanced European art decoration. He had probably studied with Alphonse Mucha in Paris, and he purchased various Secessionist-oriented periodicals such as *Die Kunst, Das Interieur,* and *Ver Sacrum.* The interior Niedecken portrayed in this drawing makes its impact from the flat planar surfaces of the walls, cabinets, and tables, which were contrasted with the intensely geometrical patterns of the rug, frieze, and upholstery. Edges and corners were emphasized, and structural supports are long and linear. Offsetting the rectilinear geometry are the graceful curves of the vaguely Art Nouveau chairs. Although this design is certainly not in the normal idiom of the Prairie architects, one can still see a sympathy of vision that indicates parallel ideals. Whether this interior design was executed is unclear; Niedecken later remodeled the gallery in 1919. Bresler and Niedecken were business associates, and Niedecken apparently purchased Japanese prints and Chinese ceramics from Bresler.

CAT. NO. 8. George Mann Niedecken
of Niedecken-Walbridge Company,
Interior Architects
*Perspective Rendering of the Proposed
Interior of the Henry Ford House,
Dearborn, Michigan,* c. 1910
Graphite and watercolor on a linen scroll;
55 x 224 cm
Restricted gift of the Thomas J. and
Mary E. Eyerman Foundation, 1984.1292

CAT. NO. 9. Frank Lloyd Wright (1867–1959)
*Triptych Window from a Niche in
the Avery Coonley Playhouse, Riverside,
Illinois,* 1912
Clear and colored glass in lead cames;
center panel: 88.9 x 109.2 cm; side panels:
each 91.4 x 19.7 cm
Restricted gift of Dr. and Mrs. Edwin J.
DeCosta, and the Walter E. Heller
Foundation, 1986.88

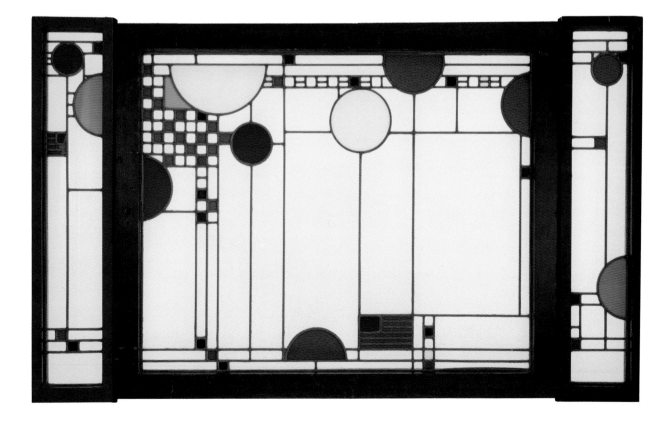

8. George Mann Niedecken of Niedecken-Walbridge Company, *Perspective Rendering of the Proposed Interior of the Henry Ford House, Dearborn, Michigan,* c. 1910

The inability of several Prairie School designers to provide a suitable house for Henry Ford in Dearborn, Michigan, must be counted as one of the great architectural tragedies of the early twentieth century. Initially Frank Lloyd Wright had negotiated with Ford on a house in 1909 before he left for Europe. But Wright had apparently never designed anything and he turned the commission over to Hermann von Holst, who in turn hired Wright's former employee Marion Mahony to design it, along with several other former Wright commissions. Around 1912 Mahony—by now married to Walter Burley Griffin—produced a design, and construction apparently began and foundations were sunk, before Ford lost interest and stopped construction. Bitter recriminations and a lawsuit ensued. Ford, who frequently expressed disdain for professionals in all fields, hired an obscure Pittsburgh architect-builder, William H. Van Tine, to complete the project. The finished house, called Fairlane, bizarrely combines a medieval Scottish baronial style with Prairie School elements. In 1914 Ford hired Jens Jensen, a Prairie School landscape architect, to design the grounds.[22]

Where this rendering by George Mann Niedecken fits into this sequence of events is unclear. It fits neither Mahony's design nor the house as built. Niedecken incorporated in the multilevel living and music room space a variety of motifs that are integrated through the employment of broad, flat surfaces of wall and ceiling paneling. The ornamental details exhibit a Secessionist manner, while the wall sconces and chandeliers are particularly Wrightian. Although the tables and cabinets have the typical heavy Prairie School flavor, the chairs seem more conventional and comfortable. As a rendering, the sheet is impressive for its sheer size and breadth of treatment.

9. Frank Lloyd Wright, *Triptych Window from a Niche in the Avery Coonley Playhouse, Riverside, Illinois,* 1912

Frank Lloyd Wright's design for this window represents one of his great triumphs of integration: an asymmetrical whole including both circular and rectilinear forms, along with an image of the American flag. Blue, red, and green circles and half circles, small clusters of black and white rectangles, and the flag are arranged in a field of large and small rectangles. Apparently Wright's design for the window was inspired by the balloons, flags, and confetti of a parade. Until this point in his career, Wright had mostly used rectilinear forms, but with this window a new period of ornamental complexity began. The window was installed in a niche in a playhouse he created for the Coonley estate in Riverside, Illinois; Wright had previously designed a

CAT. NO. 10. Walter Burley Griffin (1876–1937) and Marion Mahony Griffin (1871–1962)
Aerial Perspective View of Rock Crest/Rock Glen, Mason City, Iowa, c. 1912
Lithograph and gouache on green satin;
59 x 201 cm
Gift of Marion Mahony Griffin through Eric Nicholls, 1988.182

main house and outbuildings in 1907–08. The so-called playhouse was really a school for the Coonley's daughter, Elizabeth, and other neighborhood children that was planned along the lines of the progressive educational ideas of John Dewey. The children were involved in crafts, cooking, and study, often acting out the subjects of their more academic lessons. The principal patron of Wright's designs for the family was Mrs. Avery (Queene Ferry) Coonley (1874–1958), who observed "the countenance of principle" in his work.[23]

Born on a farm near Spring Green, Wisconsin, Wright (1867–1959) spent a peripatetic childhood living in various places prior to briefly enrolling in the engineering school at the University of Wisconsin.[24] Desiring to be an architect, he went to Chicago in 1885 and entered the office of Joseph Lyman Silsbee (1845–1913), a designer of suburban houses. In 1888 Wright joined the office of Adler and Sullivan and developed a close, though tempestuous, relationship with Sullivan. Wright left Sullivan in 1893 and established his own architectural practice with offices in Chicago and at his own house in Oak Park, to which he added a studio. Wright enjoyed remarkable early success designing not only many suburban houses in Chicago's growing western and northern suburbs but also commercial structures. By 1900 Wright's first mature style had appeared in the *Ladies Home Journal* as "A Home in a Prairie Town." Between 1900 and 1910 nearly 120 of his designs were constructed, encompassing not only houses but office buildings (like the Larkin Administration Building in Buffalo) and churches (Unity Temple in Oak Park). He developed a distinctive architectural idiom of an integrated abstract geometry that embraced space, form, and ornament. Always avid for fame and sure of his own importance, Wright pursued with remarkable success the publication of his work both at home and abroad. He was at the center of the architectural flowering in the Chicago area in these years. Beginning in 1909, Wright's personal life became tumultuous: he lived in Europe with the wife of a client, returned and sought unsuccessfully a divorce (not granted until 1922), and partially removed himself from Chicago. The Coonley Playhouse windows date from early in this period and reflect the impact of European decoration on his work.

10. Walter Burley Griffin and Marion Mahony Griffin, *Aerial Perspective View of Rock Crest/Rock Glen, Mason City, Iowa*, c. 1912

One of the greatest architectural renderings ever made in America, this bird's-eye perspective captures the flavor of the Prairie School's attitude toward the landscape. Nestled along a creek and on the surrounding roads is a small community of houses. A rough-faced limestone

quarried from the site helps to unify the diverse expression of the houses, whether it is used for the foundation, the terrace walls, or as covering for the entire house. Most of the houses are oriented so that their service facilities—kitchen, pantry, and garage—face the street, while the main living spaces and vistas open onto the creek. A large common, more properly described as a prairie river landscape, occupies the center of the site. This delicate rendering by Marion Mahony Griffin displays an oriental sensibility both in technique and form, with the long horizontal format and the division into three panels recalling Chinese scroll paintings. The vegetation, presented in flat planes, looks exotic; a golden mist hangs over the setting. Nature for the Prairie School was never wild and untamed, but always a harmonious middle landscape of domestic bliss. Pastoral in setting, the Rock Crest/Rock Glen development is quintessentially suburban; modern technology disappears and yet makes possible the reclaiming and remaking of the landscape.

The project was the product of a unique partnership between four Mason City businessmen and the team of Marion Mahony Griffin and Walter Burley Griffin. Mahony had worked for Wright as his office renderer (her monogram is in the far right panel), and she had been involved in some of his projects in Mason City during the years 1908–10. After Wright became persona non grata in Mason City because of his extramarital affairs, the businessmen approached Mahony with the idea of developing an eighteen-acre tract of land a few blocks from downtown that had served for years as a quarry and a trash dump. Mahony had recently married Walter Burley Griffin, another of Wright's former employees. As Mahony later wrote, she initially tried to beg off the job, but "the spark caught and I said I thought I could do that [make a perspective drawing] but if it was a landscape scheme he ought to talk with Mr. Griffin about it, and I showed him some of Griffin's houses, etc. He had a talk, had Griffin go down to Mason City for a day at the end of which the two gentlemen signed away their so-called liberties in a contract which bound each of them to do nothing on the property without Mr. Griffin's approval."[25] Of the sixteen houses projected in the rendering only eight were ever built, with the Griffins involved in four.

11. Walter Burley Griffin, Marion Mahony Griffin, and Augustus Fritsch, *Perspective Rendering of Newman College, University of Melbourne, Swanston Street, Melbourne, Australia*, c. 1915–17

On May 23, 1912, the judges for the design of the new capital of Australia at Canberra announced that Chicago architect Walter Burley Griffin had won the international competition. Griffin (1876–1937) was born in

CAT. NO. 11. Walter Burley Griffin, Marion
Mahony Griffin, and Augustus Fritsch
*Perspective Rendering of Newman
College, University of Melbourne, Swanston
Street, Melbourne, Australia*, c. 1915–17
Lithograph and gouache on beige satin;
48 x 118 cm
Gift of Marion Mahony Griffin through
Eric Nicholls

CAT. NO. 12. Parker Noble Berry
(1888–1918)
*Elevation Study of the Proposed Lincoln
State Bank, Chicago*, 1912
Graphite on tracing paper;
33.3 x 51.6 cm
Gift of Homer Grant Sailor, Jr., 1988.184.1

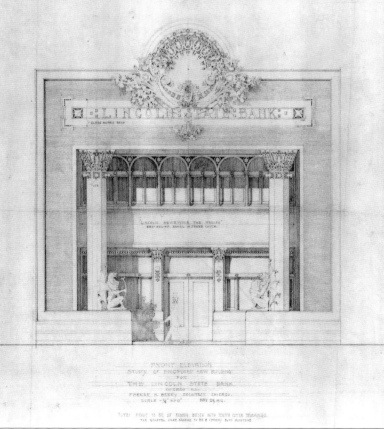

CAT. NO. 14. Designer unknown;
originally attributed to
George W. Maher (1864–1926)
*Leaded-Glass Window Depicting
a Stylized Poppy*, 1900/1915
Clear and colored glass in copper-plated
zinc cames; 168.2 x 33.4 cm
Gift of Mrs. Eugene A. Davidson, 1973.344

CAT. NO. 13. Alfonso Iannelli (1888–1965)
with Frank Lloyd Wright
*Study Model for the Head of a Sprite for
Midway Gardens, Chicago*, 1914
Plaster; 33 x 24 x 25 cm
Restricted gift of the Thomas J. and Mary E.
Eyerman Foundation, 1984.1293

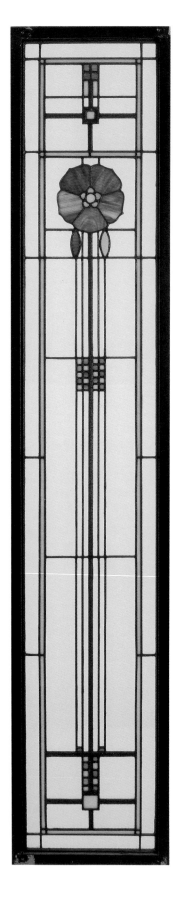

Maywood, Illinois, and he received degrees in architecture and landscape architecture at the University of Illinois. He then worked in Wright's studio from 1901 to 1905, where he met his future wife, Marion Mahony (1871–1962). Mahony was born in Chicago and received her architecture degree from MIT. She joined Wright's studio in 1895 and remained there intermittently until 1910, developing for him a distinctive rendering technique derived in part from Japanese prints. In mid-1914 Griffin and his wife permanently relocated to Australia, and he lived the remainder of his life there and in India. Only a portion of the Canberra plan saw reality, but the Griffins were sought after in Australia and designed a number of projects.

Both Griffins became interested in Theosophy and Rudolph Steiner's Anthroposophy, and some elements of the "higher consciousness" common to these spiritualist movements may have influenced the efflorescence of ornament in this scheme for Newman College at the University of Melbourne. Marion Mahony Griffin's dramatic style of rendering is fully evident in the flat foliage and tree trunks, the broad expanse of sky, and the empty center, with the major architectural activity concentrated at the periphery. The new college was intended to harmonize with the existing Gothic Revival campus. The long stretch of the arcade culminates in a large refectory with a low, hemispherical shape vaguely recalls Hagia Sophia in Istanbul. Rising from this reinforced concrete dome are spires and pinnacles, or beacons. The composition indicates that the Griffins' personal sensibility was more akin to Sullivan than to Wright; they preferred compact masses enlivened by ornament that differed dramatically from Wright's work, and their sense of the organic was multiple, unlike the singular totality favored by Wright.[26]

12. Parker Noble Berry, *Elevation Study of the Proposed Lincoln State Bank, Chicago*, 1912

Born in Hastings, Nebraska, Parker Noble Berry (1888–1918) moved as a youth to Princeton, Illinois, where his father operated a contracting business and, as a sideline, designed buildings. Berry determined at an early age to become an architect, and he designed a house for his father's business while he was still in high school. He enrolled in the architecture school at the University of Illinois but left after two years, "convinced that he was not gaining instruction in the American type of designing, which was his objective."[27] He moved to Chicago and through Kristian Schneider, who modeled much of Louis Sullivan's ornament for the American Terra Cotta Company, Berry obtained a position in Sullivan's office. Berry entered the firm in late 1909, just prior to the departure of Sullivan's chief designer, George Grant

Elmslie. Shortly thereafter Berry assumed this role, staying with Sullivan until 1917. Commissions were few for Sullivan in these years, and Berry was frequently the only employee. As a result, Berry worked on all the projects in Sullivan's office in these years: among them the People's Savings Bank (1909–11) and St. Paul's Methodist Episcopal Church (1910–11) in Cedar Rapids, Iowa; the Henry C. Adams Building (1913) in Algona, Iowa; the Merchants National Bank (1913–14) in Grinnell, Iowa; the John D. Van Allen and Sons Store (1913–15) in Clinton, Iowa; and the People's Savings and Loan Association Building (1917) in Sidney, Ohio. At the same time Berry worked nights and weekends on his own projects, which included a bank in his hometown of Princeton in 1915, and a bank on the South Side of Chicago in the Polish-American community of Hegewisch in 1917–18 (now demolished). In addition, Berry built a few other designs, such as an addition to a retirement home in Princeton in 1917, before he succumbed to influenza during the epidemic of 1918.

This design by Berry from 1912 is contemporary with Sullivan's Grinnell bank, and contains similar elements, such as the winged lions. The layering of the facade, with the deep entrance panel, recalls the Algona building, while the arched windows look back to Sullivan's designs of the 1890s, especially the Bayard and Guaranty buildings in New York and Buffalo. At the same time, the great florescence of ornament that rises above the cornice line is a creative departure that Sullivan never attempted. The ornament, though of course typically Sullivanesque, illuminates Berry's facility. Another noteworthy aspect of this composition is Berry's inclusion of side panels.

13. Alfonso Iannelli with Frank Lloyd Wright, *Study Model for the Head of a Sprite for Midway Gardens, Chicago*, 1914

Severe, geometrical, and enigmatic, this sprite head served as a model for a series of sculptural embellishments at Midway Gardens. In 1913 Frank Lloyd Wright received a commission from the son of an old client, Edward Waller, Jr., to design an entertainment garden, a place not unlike a European beer garden or casino, where music and dancing could take place as the guests ate and drank. In designing an enormous complex taking up two city blocks, Wright created a series of indoor and outdoor spaces constructed out of a decorative concrete block. Wright's growing ornamental sensibility in these years became fully evident in this project's overall patterning, elaborate stanchions, and murals. Completed in 1914 on Chicago's South Side, the vast complex never proved economically viable; Waller sold it within two years, and Prohibition brought its death knell. Midway Gardens was demolished in 1929.[28]

CAT. NO. 15. Barry Byrne (1883–1967)
with Alfonso Iannelli
*Perspective Rendering of the Exterior
of St. Francis Xavier High School,
Wilmette, Illinois,* 1922–23
Graphite on tracing paper; 41.5 x 66 cm
Restricted gift of the Thomas J. and
Mary E. Eyerman Foundation, 1984.1298

The various sculptural figures of Midway Gardens were among its most distinctive features, and were the products of a collaboration between Wright and Alfonso Iannelli. The debate over the source and design of the figures has been somewhat contentious, since Wright may have seen a similar type of figure in Vienna during his European sojourn of 1909–10.[29] But Wright himself never mentioned this possibility, claiming rather that his employment of "the straight line, square, triangle and circle" was the source for the architecture, its painting, and the sculptures. He acknowledged, however, that the "Mona Lisa smile" was the contribution of Iannelli, though this admission came years later.[30] Ultimately, they worked as collaborators, and the assignment of total responsibility to one or the other is impossible, since Iannelli's work prior to the Midway commission bears a striking resemblance to what he produced here.

Born in Italy, Alfonso Iannelli (1888–1965) came to the United States at the age of ten and trained at the Newark (New Jersey) Technical School and then at the Art Student's League in New York under Gutzon Borglum. Working as a sculptor, decorator, and commercial artist, Iannelli developed an interest in creating an "American art."[31] After settling in Los Angeles in 1910, he designed a series of theater posters that indicated his awareness of the Vienna Secession. These posters, done between 1910 and 1913, with their abstract, flat, and planar human forms point directly to the Midway sculptures. While in California, Iannelli met Wright's two oldest sons (Lloyd and John Lloyd), who worked in architects' offices in the area, as well as Barry Byrne, and through these connections Wright brought Iannelli back to Chicago. But Wright omitted Iannelli's name from the credits for Midway Gardens, and they never collaborated again. Iannelli though did remain in Chicago, frequently working with Barry Byrne (see cat. no. 15), Purcell and Elmslie, Bruce Goff, and John Lloyd Wright.

14. Designer unknown, originally attributed to George W. Maher, *Leaded-Glass Window Depicting a Stylized Poppy,* 1900/1915

This dramatic window has long been attributed to George Washington Maher (1864–1926), a leading member of the Prairie School, but recent research makes this appear unlikely. Nonetheless, it represents the type of art glass turned out by Chicago stained-glass companies such as Drehobl Brothers, Flanagan and Biedenweg, Giannini and Hilgart, and Schuler and Mueller for Prairie-style residences.[32] The window has a composition mindful of Maher's theories and also the "Pure Design" movement that interested many Chicago designers during this period. Essentially, the window is composed of a series of rectilinear forms of different sizes. Long, vertical rectangles are offset by small squares that are attached to the spine of the window and balance the five-leafed poppy and bud shapes immediately below.

This combination of geometrical and floral elements is a good example of Maher's theory of design, called "motif-rhythm," by which he would choose a plant or a shape to be used throughout a building, both in its overall form and ornamental details. Maher's basic rectilinear form was enlivened and related to the surroundings through the use of motifs from nature. The motif-rhythm appears in one of Maher's designs that is open to the public, the John Farson House, or "Pleasant Home," of 1897 in Oak Park, where the thistle motif abounds (see cat. no. 35).

Born in Mill Creek, West Virginia, Maher began as an architect's apprentice at the age of thirteen, and he later worked in the office of Joseph Lyman Silsbee, where a number of other Prairie School designers also trained. From 1888 Maher—except for brief partnerships—was on his own until after World War I when he joined with his son, Philip. He fiercely advocated, and was one of the principal spokesmen for, a new American architecture, and he was extremely prolific, designing over 300 works in a long career.[33] Maher followed neither the Sullivan nor the Wright wing of the Prairie School, and instead pursued an independent course. From a beginning greatly influenced by H. H. Richardson, Maher did change his architectural idiom over time, and he was extensively influenced after 1905 by the Vienna Secessionists and the English domestic architect and designer Charles F. A. Voysey. But he also maintained a tie to the classical principles of composition, as can be seen in his more public works at Northwestern University in Evanston and in Winona, Minnesota. Most of his architecture, however, remained at the domestic scale, and he designed many houses in Evanston, Glencoe, Kenilworth, and other Chicago suburbs.

15. Barry Byrne with Alfonso Iannelli, *Perspective Rendering of the Exterior of St. Francis Xavier High School, Wilmette, Illinois,* 1922–23

Born Francis Barry Byrne (1883–1967) in Chicago, Barry Byrne received his architectural training in the Oak Park studio of Frank Lloyd Wright between 1902 and 1908.[34] He practiced briefly in Seattle with another Wright protégé and then in California for a short period before returning to Chicago in 1913. He took over from Walter Burley Griffin and Marion Mahony Griffin—who were preparing to leave for Australia—the Rock Crest/Rock Glen project in Mason City, Iowa (see cat. no. 10), for which he designed several houses. On his return to Chicago, Byrne also began a long-term association with Alfonso Iannelli (see cat. no. 13); Iannelli designed sculptural embellishments and murals for Byrne's projects, and they collaborated on product design. In the early 1920s Byrne embarked on a long career as a designer of Roman Catholic churches and schools, a series of commissions that would carry him into the 1950s. But in the 1920s his work in this vein met with some resistance because both the Catholic Church and the leader of the Chicago Archdiocese, Cardinal Mundelein, disapproved of modernism.

This design for St. Francis Xavier High School at 808 Linden Avenue in Wilmette illustrates how certain aspects of the Prairie School continued into the 1920s and beyond. In spite of being trained by Wright, Byrne had a proclivity toward space-enclosing, solid boxy forms enlivened by applied ornament that was inspired by Louis Sullivan. He rejected Wright's interweaving of intersecting space-defining rectangles with integrated ornament. The eccentric fenestration of rotated cubes and tall, pointed arches recalls some of the midwestern banks that Sullivan designed late in his career, as well as his insertion of disparate forms into cubical masses. At the same time, however, Byrne's angular geometry also may reflect the impact of Iannelli, who in fact contributed the sculptured figures in the corners and the decorative coping on this school. Shortly after their work together on this design, Byrne and Iannelli spent several months in Europe, and both became interested in the work of Dutch and German Expressionists: Hendrikus Theodorus Wijdeveld, Pieter Kramer, Michel de Klerk, Hans Poelzig, and Erich Mendelsohn. Byrne's own later work shifts even more toward the Expressionist stance that was already apparent in this work for St. Xavier. At the same time the decorative features and the fractured geometry of St. Xavier is reminiscent of contemporary American modernist work of the 1920s, or Art Deco, and thus indicates another legacy of the Prairie School. The rendering itself, with its flat vegetation and thin, delicate line, resembles drawings of Marion Mahony (see cat. nos. 10–11).

THE PRAIRIE SCHOOL AND DECORATIVE ARTS
AT THE ART INSTITUTE OF CHICAGO

JUDITH A. BARTER

Field-McCormick Curator of American Arts
The Art Institute of Chicago

From the Chicago architectural practice of Louis H. Sullivan came a philosophy that emphasized organic naturalism. Eschewing historical revivalism, Sullivan taught that "form follows function"—that architecture should correspond to the example of the natural world where the forms of plants and animals reflected their ability to survive, reproduce, and endure. For Sullivan, and his Prairie School followers, the designs and materials of architecture reflected the meaning or function of the building itself.[1]

Sullivan's philosophy of naturalism often took on a spiritual quality in the works of his followers. This was not the neo-medievalism or handicraft practice of William Morris and the Arts and Crafts movement. To be sure, the Prairie School architects and their designs were influenced early on by the English Arts and Crafts movement, and its counterpart, the Chicago Arts and Crafts Society founded in 1897 at Jane Addams's progressive Hull House. But unlike many Arts and Crafts reformers, Sullivan's disciples welcomed the machine as an integral and formative part of twentieth-century life and aesthetics. What was spiritual and reflective in the works of Prairie School architects was not a handicraft process, but rather the process of design itself. The central design concept permeated every aspect of planning and unified the whole. Each of the Prairie School architects and designers was drawn to systematic designs and to the total integration of all parts of an architectural plan and the built environment. As Professor Louis J. Millet of The School of The Art Institute of Chicago stated in 1899, "I believe the day is dawning when . . . almost all . . . of the furniture in the home will be built for that building, and for no

other. Then it will fit; then it will harmonize with the architectural design of the place and with the decorative scheme of the coloring."[2]

This emphasis on a unified design had its counterpart in Asian art forms. The popularity of Japanese prints among many Prairie School practitioners was understandable in light of such thinking. What appealed to architects like Frank Lloyd Wright, William Gray Purcell, George Grant Elmslie, and George W. Maher about Japanese design was its combination of positive and negative space, its reduction of form to its simplest essence, and its unification of the temporal and the spiritual.[3]

Unlike Sullivan, who abstracted ornament in order to evoke nature,[4] Wright and his Prairie School colleagues concentrated on space itself. Quoting from Okakura Kakuzo's *Book of Tea,* Wright wrote, "The reality of a room was to be found in the space enclosed by the roof and walls, not by the roof and walls themselves."[5] By organic Wright meant "an architecture that *develops* from within outward in harmony with the conditions of its being, as distinguished from one that is *applied* from without."[6]

In his paper "In the Cause of Architecture" (1908), Wright called the new practitioners of the totally integrated built environment the "New School of the Middle West."[7] The phrase indicates that Wright and his colleagues

FACING PAGE, TOP: Frank Lloyd Wright, c. 1905. Photo courtesy of the Frank Lloyd Wright Home and Studio Foundation.

FACING PAGE, BOTTOM: George Feick, Jr., William Gray Purcell, and George Grant Elmslie in their office, 1910. Photo courtesy of the Northwest Architectural Archives, University of Minnesota Libraries, St. Paul.

were aware of the place-specific nature of their work. Indeed, the Prairie School architects and craftsmen, such as Maher and Robert Riddle Jarvie, turned to the nature found in the Midwest, and to American Indian motifs, for some of their inspiration. Contemporary architects noted the preference for straight lines and horizontal planes that were equated to the unrelenting horizontality of the landscape—one reflected in the low-slung, broad roof lines and masses of Prairie houses.[8]

Finally, "Prairie School" as a label applied to architecture and the decorative arts was time-specific as well. The inspiration of the prairie was more than just visual. It represented newness, and a sense of experimentation, like a broad, unwritten page.

In a serialized story that began in the December 1901 issue of *Ladies Home Journal*, Emily Wheaton recounted the adventures of "The Russells in Chicago, the Experiences of a Young Boston couple who Move to the West." On a trip east, Ned Russell finds that he is eager to return to Chicago:

[He] had been inoculated with the virus of the West, and it had taken so successfully that he was forever weaned from all

Eastern conventionality and conservatism. He longed to get back again where he had room to grow and spread out; he loved the whole breezy, energetic atmosphere; he felt the force and strength of the West, and was eager to plunge into the thick of the smoke, the noise and the din of the battle of Life.

The kind of particularly midwestern and innovative style that Ned Russell found to his liking in Chicago reflected the new architectural ideas and the spirit of progressive reform prevalent during the first two decades of the new century. Prairie School design emerged from English Arts and Crafts ideals and was fueled by modernism to become a geographically and temporally specific movement of far-reaching importance.

16. David Wolcott Kendall, *Armchair*, 1894/96

The spirit of reform, for creating a new age and a new place, was seen not just in Chicago, but throughout the Midwest. In Grand Rapids, Michigan, the major furniture-producing center of the nation, David Wolcott Kendall designed unadorned furniture that could be easily manufactured by machine.[9] His stained oak armchair, first

CAT. NO. 16. David Wolcott Kendall
(1851–1910)
Phoenix Furniture Company,
Grand Rapids, Michigan
Armchair, 1894/96
Green-stained oak with caned inserts;
86 x 75 x 56 cm
Gift of the Antiquarian Society through
Morris and Jane Weeden, 1995.101

CAT. NO. 17. J. S. Ford, Johnson and
Company
Armchair, 1904–05
Brown-stained oak; 81 x 52 x 50 cm
Restricted gift of Henry and Gilda
Buchbinder, 1995.100

designed for the Phoenix Furniture Company around 1895, was an early departure from the heavily carved walnut and mahogany furniture then prevalent. The caned seat adds lightness to the already spare, geometric simplicity of the design. Except for the gothic-arched detailing, which points to its nineteenth-century origins, this modern-looking chair could well have been made during the 1920s.

When introduced to the market in the mid-1890s, this chair was named for President William McKinley, who was presented with a prototype for his offices at the White House.[10] The McKinley chair was one of Kendall's most successful endeavors, gaining him praise from the furniture manufacturing community for its forward-looking design. Books and magazines from the early twentieth century reveal that the chair was still used in a variety of settings for decades after it was first produced.[11] Kendall's chair perhaps influenced Frank Lloyd Wright's geometric, caned birch chairs for the Sherman Booth House (1912; Glencoe, Illinois), which are now in the collection of the Chicago Historical Society.

In the nineteenth century, high-style furniture was primarily crafted out of mahogany, walnut, and rose-

wood. Oak was thought of as a common material, lacking the dark rich color and smooth grain characteristic of the more expensive woods. But because of the increasing scarcity of walnut and the prohibitive expense of mahogany, Kendall turned to oak, which could be had in abundance from the forests of Indiana. At first, Kendall developed a number of brightly colored finishes, like yellow, copper, and malachite green, which hid the oak used in his furniture. Later, Kendall set out to develop a series of stains that would darken the color of the wood and highlight the open grain. Because of his immense success, other manufacturers designed oak furniture and copied finishes developed by Kendall.[12] His most imitated stain, known as the "Belgian finish," was used on this chair. Its green color was used in textiles, ceramics, metalwork, and other furniture of the period.[13]

17. J. S. Ford, Johnson and Company, *Armchair,* 1904–05

Headquartered in Chicago, with divisions in Indiana and Massachusetts, J. S. Ford, Johnson and Company was one of the largest chair manufacturers in the country. It was one of several Chicago-based furniture manufacturing businesses that expanded its scope of operations at the end of the nineteenth century to include all steps of production, from cutting trees to placing chairs on the showroom floor.[14] During the mid-1880s, the company showcased more than three thousand varieties of chairs, and used interchangeable parts.[15] Ford, Johnson used such parts to maintain its vast selection of designs.[16] From the start, the company was mostly involved in producing lines of office furniture, but by the turn of the century several new styles, such as this chair, were introduced for residential use.

This design, numbered 3051, was introduced in the 1904–05 trade catalogue as part of a suite of furniture that also included a settee and a rocking chair. A customer could purchase an individual chair or the entire suite.[17] Several different versions could be had: a plain style, like the Art Institute's chair; one with a strapped-down cushion; and one with an upholstered seat and back. Though the chairs were mass-produced, the exposed wooden rivets reveal an affinity with hand craftsmanship, and form a connection to California coppersmith Dirk Van Erp's designs.[18] The bold, crisp lines of the chair were also inspired by the work of two other European designers who produced similar chairs, the Englishman Robert Oerley in 1899 and the German-born Joseph Urban in 1902.[19] The creation of such a fresh, artistic design by a firm that mass-produced over three thousand different chair designs, mostly institutional ones, illustrates the skill of the firm's designers and the impetus toward a simplified, organic, modern style developing in Chicago and the Midwest.[20]

18. George W. Maher, *Library Table*, c. 1905

George Washington Maher was born in 1864 in Mill Creek, West Virginia, and moved with his family to New Albany, Indiana, and then to Chicago shortly after the 1871 fire. At the age of thirteen he entered an architectural apprenticeship in the firm of two German immigrant architects, Augustus Bauer and Henry W. Hill. During the 1880s Maher worked in the office of Joseph Lyman Silsbee, where he was exposed to new philosophies of residential design work. By 1888 the young Maher had opened his own office.

Maher's Chicago-area residences, including the John Farson House in Oak Park (1897; see cat. no. 35), the

FIGURE 1. George W. Maher. *Armchair*, 1897. Commissioned for the John Farson House, Oak Park, Illinois. Mahogany; 129.7 x 76.3 x 63.6 cm. The Art Institute of Chicago, Lent by the Park District of Oak Park (72.1971).

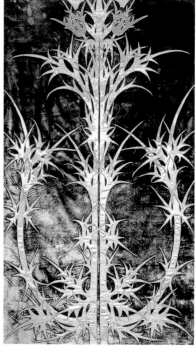

James Patten House in Evanston (1901), and the Emil Rudolph House in Highland Park (1905), exhibit symmetrical, classically inspired facades, but devoid of classical ornament or detail. Their horizontal masses and abstracted, geometric leaded-glass windows show a Prairie School sensibility. Indeed, Maher's philosophy of architecture—function should determine design—was in keeping with that of his Chicago colleagues.

Maher published his "motif-rhythm" theory, which explained his working method. He combined a geometric shape with a stylized flower to create a decorative theme that he repeated throughout each of his buildings, thus unifying interior and exterior elements.[21]

Maher did not design furniture for all his houses, but did so for larger commissions such as the Farson and the Rudolph houses. At the Farson House, Maher com-bined honeysuckle motifs with lions' heads throughout the building and on the dining-room chairs (fig. 1). The chairs retain a heavily ornamented, richly carved, massive quality no doubt influenced by Maher's association with Germanic architecture.

By the time Maher designed the Rudolph House, he had moved away from the monumentality of the Farson furniture. He had seen the modern Austrian and German exhibits at the 1904 St. Louis World's Fair[22] and was familiar with the designs of C. F. A. Voysey, Charles Rennie Mackintosh and the Vienna Secessionist group, all illustrated in *The Studio* magazine between 1897 and 1905. Maher's thistle design for the James A. Patten House (figs. 2–3) reflects the influence of Voysey's textile patterns and is more florid and curvaceous than his later work. The use of the thistle pattern was also related

CAT. NO. 19. George Grant Elmslie
(1871–1952) of Purcell, Feick and Elmslie,
Architects, Minneapolis
Side Chair, 1910
Possibly from the Mrs. T. B. Keith House,
Eau Claire, Wisconsin
Oak, laminated wood, leather, jute webbing
and horsehair (original upholstery);
127.3 x 48.9 x 41.2 cm
Mrs. William P. Boggess II Fund, 1973.342

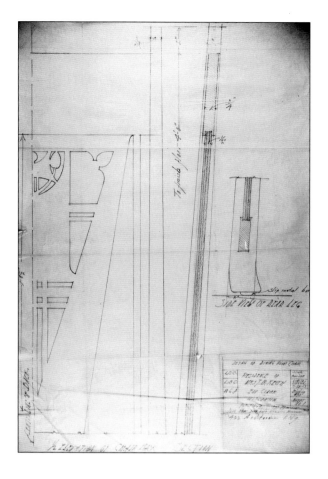

to Patten's Scottish ancestry and to the fact that thistles grew wild on the building site.[23] (This and other Prairie School textiles are housed in the Department of Textiles at The Art Institute of Chicago.)

For the Rudolph House, Maher chose the tulip as a decorative motif. The oak library table features the flower in a linen-fold type of carving that is reminiscent of English Arts and Crafts work. The motif was repeated in the glass windows, the bookcases, the fireplace mosaic, the dining sconces, the newel post, and the stair banisters. The attenuated verticality of Maher's motif is balanced by the long, wide, horizontal emphasis of the table. Center supports maintain Maher's interest in a stripped-down, reinterpreted classicism.

19. George Grant Elmslie, *Side Chair,* 1910

George Grant Elmslie was born in Scotland and emigrated to Chicago with his family in 1884. In 1887 he studied architecture in the office of Joseph Lyman Silsbee, where the staff included George Maher and Frank Lloyd Wright. By 1889 Wright joined the office of Louis Sullivan, and persuaded Elmslie to join him. Wright left the firm by the mid-1890s, and Elmslie became Sullivan's chief draftsman for the next fifteen years. As Sullivan's trusted colleague, Elmslie translated Sullivan's ideas into finished designs. Elmslie designed the ironwork entrance and the

ABOVE: FIGURE 5. George Grant Elmslie of Purcell, Feick and Elmslie. *Full-Size Detail of Dining Chair for the Mrs. T. B. Keith House, Eau Claire, Wisconsin,* 1910. Photo courtesy of the Northwest Architectural Archives, William Gray Purcell Papers, University of Minnesota Libraries, St. Paul.

LEFT: FIGURE 4. Purcell, Feick and Elmslie. Dining room in E. L. Powers House, Minneapolis, 1916. Photo: *Western Architect* 19, 1 (Jan. 1913), p. 19.

FIGURE 6. George Grant Elmslie of Purcell, Feick and Elmslie. Face of *Tall Clock* (cat. no. 20); cast bronze face modeled by Kristian Schneider; original hands made by Robert Riddle Jarvie. Photo: *Western Architect* 22, 1 (July 1915), p. 9.

CAT. NO. 20. George Grant Elmslie of Purcell, Feick and Elmslie, Architects, Minneapolis
Tall Clock, 1912
From the Henry Babson House, Riverside, Illinois
Manufactured by the firm of Niedecken-Walbridge, Milwaukee
Mahogany with brass inlay;
213.3 x 66 x 40 cm
Restricted gift of Mrs. Theodore D. Tieken, 1971.322

modular five-ply sawn-wood screens for the Schlesinger and Mayer (now Carson Pirie Scott and Company) department store in Chicago (1900–1903).[24]

Elmslie hired the Oak Park native William Gray Purcell in 1903. Purcell left the firm after five months, but the friendship between the two men continued. As early as 1907 Purcell and Elmslie corresponded about Purcell's residential designs, and in 1909 Elmslie left Sullivan's office to join Purcell and his Cornell classmate George Feick, Jr., in Minneapolis. The partnership of Purcell, Feick and Elmslie lasted until Feick's departure in 1913, after which the firm was known simply as Purcell and Elmslie.[25]

Purcell, devoted to the theory of organic architecture, rendered his ideas in notes and drawings that delineated the overall structure. Feick attended to specifications and engineering problems. Elmslie translated these ideas into detailed graphic designs, and usually provided the drawings for furniture, terracotta, leaded glass panels, stencils, and other decorative arts.

While still in the employ of Sullivan, Elmslie designed a series of armchairs for residential use. Variations of tall-backed side chairs with cut-out splats were used at the Harold C. Bradley House (1909; Madison, Wisconsin; now Sigma Phi Alpha Society House of Wisconsin); the E. L. Powers House (1910; Minneapolis; see fig. 4); the Mrs. T. B. Keith House (1910; Eau Claire, Wisconsin); the Amy Hamilton Hunter House (1916; Minneapolis); and as a wedding gift for Bonnie Hunter Elmslie.[26] In the Powers House, the tall-backed chairs surrounded a circular oak table that was mounted on an intersecting geometric base. The details of the space were tied together by the triangular, geometric motif—chair back, pedestal base, wall stenciling—that echoed the abstract motif of the inverted triangle and the play between positive and negative space. Terracotta detail in the front entrance and the sawn-wood design of the front door of the Powers residence continued the motif.

An oral provenance linked this chair to the Charles Purcell House in River Forest, Illinois (1909), but there is no documentary evidence that Elmslie designed furnishings for the house of his future partner's father. However, an Elmslie drawing for the Mrs. T. B. Keith House dated June 1910 (fig. 5), which is now in the collection of the Northwest Architectural Archives at the University of Minnesota Libraries in St. Paul, Minnesota, matches exactly the pattern of the Art Institute's side chair.[27]

The rectilinearity used in Elmslie's designs was also favored by other Prairie School architects such as Wright and European designers such as Charles Rennie Mackintosh.[28] Elmslie's chair designs show a strongly graphic sensibility.

20–21. George Grant Elmslie, *Tall Clock* and *Andirons*, 1912

George Grant Elmslie had been responsible for the built-in and freestanding furnishings of the Henry Babson House in Riverside, Illinois (1907), while still employed as Louis Sullivan's chief designer. In 1912 Babson asked Purcell and Elmslie to design eight pieces of furniture for this same structure.[29] One of these was a tall clock for a corner in the entrance hallway. Illustrated in *The Western Architect* in July 1915 (fig. 6), the clock contained a cast-bronze face modeled by Chicago's Kristian Schneider, and the original hands were made by Chicago Arts and Crafts metalsmith Robert Riddle Jarvie.[30]

Made of mahogany, the case front is pierced by the familiar sawn-wood decorative technique favored by Elmslie. The piercing allows a view of the pendulum. The clock reflects the predilection of Purcell and Elmslie for decorative harmony—a basic geometric form, usually rectilinear, tempered by a flowing, organic motif drawn from nature. The rectilinear severity, perhaps inspired by Japanese temples, is softened by the four-part, sawn-wood design that repeats curling, natural tendrils arranged in subtle rotation.

Among the decorative motifs used at the Babson House, the four-part division emerges again in the fireplace andirons designed for the hearth adjacent to what was the sleeping porch. The original sleeping porch was closed in during the 1912–14 renovations. The glass doors of the porch illustrated in the July 1915 issue of *The Western Architect* (fig. 7) show the unified decorative plan. The motif on the andirons matches that of the doors. The andirons themselves are barely visible through the doors. A third work from the Babson House in the Art Institute's collection is a carpet designed by Elmslie (fig. 8).

Henry Babson tried unsuccessfully to sell his house to the town of Riverside around 1960. Before the house was demolished, interior fittings, windows, and furnishings were salvaged.

22. Purcell, Feick and Elmslie, *Armchair*, 1911–12

Although most of the Purcell, Feick and Elmslie work was residential, the firm designed some municipal buildings and banks. One of the most successful of their public commissions was the Merchants Bank of Winona, Minnesota (fig. 9), completed between 1911 and 1912. Eschewing the traditional bank forms based on Greek and Roman temple architecture, Purcell, Feick and Elmslie relied on a combination of boxy steel structures with brick facades, terracotta ornament, and strongly geometric, horizontal, and integrated interiors. Lighting fixtures, tellers' cages with metal grilles, interior and exterior ornament, and furniture all harmonized around a central design

CAT. NO. 21. George Grant Elmslie of Purcell, Feick and Elmslie, Architects, Minneapolis
Andirons, 1912
From the Henry Babson House, Riverside, Illinois
Brass, bronze, and cast iron; 26.5 x 20 x 72.4 cm each
Gift of Mrs. George A. Harvey, 1971.788 a-b

theme.[31] The original rendering for the Merchants Bank, published in the January 1913 issue of *The Western Architect,* shows a two-story, square box compartmentalized into public and private spaces: a central lobby surrounded by offices and conference rooms.

This chair, one of a set of eight designed for the directors' boardroom, represents a new modular, geometric expression for the firm. It exudes a comfortable formality appropriate to a boardroom, and echoes the tellers' desks and grilles of the main banking room. Some scholars have pointed out the parallels between these cube-like chairs and the designs of Austrian Secessionist Koloman Moser.[32] Similar chairs were used in the bank's waiting room, but those chairs lacked the raised back-rail extensions and had slightly narrower back rests. Variations on this design also were used in several of the Purcell, Feick and Elmslie houses, but were of slightly different proportions and without feet.

23–24. Robert Riddle Jarvie, *Candlesticks,* 1905/15, and *Pitcher,* 1911; *Punch Bowl, Ladle, and Tray,* 1911

Robert Riddle Jarvie was a self-taught metalsmith who showed his work at the Chicago Arts and Crafts Society in the early years of the century. He exhibited candlesticks and lanterns in the Chicago Arts and Crafts Society's 1900 exhibition and soon came to public notice. At the same time he advertised in the Chicago publication *House Beautiful* as "the Candlestick Maker."[33] Jarvie fashioned the majority of his candlesticks in copper or cast bronze, and patinated their surfaces with brush polishing and acids to produce a green finish. The Art Institute owns a pair of Jarvie's thick, tubular, hammered copper candle-

sticks as well as this attenuated pair of silver candlesticks (cat. no. 23), which suggest a continuity and harmony between candlestick and candle.[34] The elongated sticks also take their inspiration from natural flower forms, reflecting the influence of the English Arts and Crafts movement. Jarvie's candlestick designs were elegant in geometry and proportion and were widely, if less successfully, imitated.

By 1905 he had opened the Jarvie Shop in the Fine Arts Building in Chicago, and in 1912 he moved his workshop to the Old English Cottage Building at the Chicago Stockyards.[35] There he fashioned trophies commissioned by Stockyards President Arthur G. Leonard to be given as awards at stockyard events. His presentation silver is some of his most innovative work. Besides the Chicago Society of Arts and Crafts, Jarvie was associated with the Cliff Dwellers Club, an association of artists, writers, musicians, and architects, among whose charter members was Art Institute President Charles H. Hutchinson. Jarvie was commissioned by the club to make a silver punch bowl (cat. no. 24). For the Cliff Dwellers, he appropriately borrowed decorative motifs from Indian coiled baskets to produce an innovative design.[36] In the boldness of its footed form and broad expanses of unadorned surface, the Art Institute's Jarvie silver punch bowl is indebted to English Arts and Crafts designers such as C. R. Ashbee. Its rectilinear, abstract decoration, however, reflects Jarvie's knowledge of the spare, linear fretwork designs of fellow Scotsman Charles Rennie Mackintosh. Jarvie's work after 1911, especially in trophies and presentation pieces is more closely tied to the geometric and abstract than to the naturalistic.

Jarvie's silver water pitcher, a wedding gift, incorpo-

FIGURE 7. Purcell, Feick and Elmslie,
architects. Sitting room doors for
Henry B. Babson House, Riverside,
Illinois, 1912. Photo: *Western Architect* 22,
1 (July 1915), pl. 5.

FIGURE 8. George Grant Elmslie. *Carpet
for Henry B. Babson House, Riverside,
Illinois,* 1908/12. Linen, cotton, and wool,
plain weave with "Ghiordes knots"
cut pile; 560.1 x 115.7 cm. The Art Institute
of Chicago, Restricted Gift of Mrs.
Theodore Tieken (1972.1144).

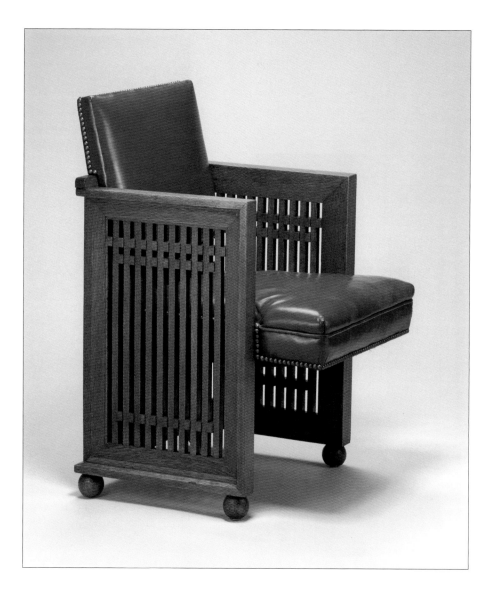

CAT. NO. 22. William Gray Purcell
(1880–1964), George Feick, Jr. (1881–1945),
and George Grant Elmslie of Purcell, Feick
and Elmslie, Architects, Minneapolis
Armchair, 1911–12
From the Merchants Bank, Winona,
Minnesota
Oak, with original green leather upholstery
and brass tacks; 92.7 x 61.6 x 65.4 cm
Mr. and Mrs. Manfred Steinfeld Fund,
1985.777

FIGURE 9. Purcell, Feick and Elmslie.
Interior of the Merchants Bank, Winona,
Minnesota, 1911–12. Photo: *Western
Architect* 21, 1 (Jan. 1915), pl. 13.

CAT. NO. 23. Robert Riddle Jarvie
(1865–1941)
Candlesticks, 1905/15
Silver; 35.7 x 8.1 cm
Bessie Bennett and Mrs. Herbert Stern
funds, 1973.377–378

Pitcher, 1911
Silver; 26 x 20.3 cm; 16 cm diam. base
Engraved inscription on the underside:
PRESENTED TO / CHARLOTTE AILEEN HENRY
/ ON HER WEDDING DAY / OCTOBER THE
TENTH / NINETEEN HUNDRED AND ELEVEN /
BY / ALBERT AND MARY GRAY / ROBERT
AND LILLIAN JARVIE / SAMUEL AND
WINIFRED GRACIE / JAMES WILBUR GRAY
and Made by the Shop of Robert Jarvie
Chicago / STERLING
Gift of Raymond W. Sheets, 1973.357

CAT. NO. 24. Robert Riddle Jarvie
Punch Bowl, Ladle, and Tray, 1911
Silver; punch bowl: 25.7 x 39.3 cm; ladle:
45.7 cm; tray: 1.9 x 52.7 cm
Embossed on rim: PRESENTED TO JOHN H.
HATTSTAEDT BY THE FACULTY OF THE
AMERICAN CONSERVATORY OF MUSIC ON
THE TWENTY-FIFTH ANNIVERSARY OF ITS
FOUNDATION . . . 1886–1911
Gift of Mr. and Mrs John R. Hattstaedt
in memory of his father, John J. Hattstaedt,
1974.293 a–c

rates the bride's initials, C.A.H., in an inverted heart
within an embossed, Celtic-inspired design (cat. no. 23).
The interlaced motif upon a stippled ground is perfectly
balanced; the curve of the heart echoes the sweeping
handle. Applied, interlaced strapwork designs were
favored by Chicago metalsmiths.

Jarvie's ornamental style is draftsmanlike, possibly
reflecting the influence of his friend and colleague
George Grant Elmslie. Indeed, Jarvie's design on this
pitcher is similar in feeling to some of the simplified
arabesques, and interlaced, abstracted designs Elmslie
produced for the Babson House the following year.[37]

Jarvie went out of business sometime between 1917
and 1920. He was employed at C. D. Peacock, a Chicago
jewelry store, until his retirement in the 1930s to the
Scottish Old People's Home, where he died in 1941.

25. Kalo Shop, *Water Pitcher,* 1910

Founded by Clara P. Barck in 1900, the original Kalo
Shop was one of the earliest silversmithing enterprises in
Chicago. Barck graduated from the School of the Art
Institute and chose the name Kalo, a Greek word meaning beauty, for the name of her shop. After her marriage
in 1905, she became Clara Barck Welles and moved her
craft community to rural Park Ridge, Illinois, still main-
taining a retail shop downtown. At the height of the
shop's operation, twenty-five artisans were employed—
both men and women, for Welles was an advocate of
women's involvement in the Arts and Crafts movement.
Welles served as designer, teacher, and smith; and the
shop's production included pitchers, bowls, trays, desk
accessories, and jewelry in copper, brass, and silver.

The overall simplicity and hammered texture of early Kalo silver bespeaks its Arts and Crafts philosophical and aesthetic origins, yet the bold, geometric modern shape of this pitcher shows the influence of Prairie School aesthetics. Like the Prairie School architects who designed machine-made furniture, the Kalo Shop favored the look of hand-raised silver but often fashioned objects from machine-rolled sheets of metal. This seamed pitcher was fashioned in this way.

Early Kalo designs show the influence of the Englishman C. R. Ashbee's Guild of Handicraft. Products from Ashbee's guild were exhibited at the Art Institute in 1898, and two years later he lectured at the Art Institute.[38] Ashbee favored paneled designs such as this pitcher, and this motif is often found in Chicago art silver.[39] Like Robert Riddle Jarvie's work, the ornament is well integrated and balanced with the body of the object. The intertwined initials, which subtly echo the overall silhouette of the piece, were a favorite Prairie School decorative device.

26. Frank Lloyd Wright, *Library Table*, 1896

Like those of his Prairie School colleagues, Frank Lloyd Wright's principles of architecture and design developed from the English Arts and Crafts movement. The Prairie architects shared the Arts and Crafts philosophy of simplicity of design, visually understandable construction, and plain, high-quality materials. Wright differed from the artisanal nature of his English colleagues, however, in that he championed the use of machinery in making well-designed objects.

Wright became a charter member of the Chicago Arts and Crafts Society in 1897, and, like other Arts and Crafts practitioners, he lamented the decline of craftsmanship and good design. Many English and American proponents of the Arts and Crafts philosophy advocated a return to medieval design inspiration and handcrafted work as the only solution. By 1901, however, Wright believed that machinery could be used to simplify and improve design. His radical departure from traditional Arts and Crafts philosophy was summarized in his now famous address entitled "The Art and Craft of the Machine."[40]

Wright believed that the machine could be used to simplify design, and strip it of unnecessary ornament. He also maintained that the machine could be used to preserve the nature of materials and that beauty was drawn from design itself. Wright's library table designed for the remodeling of the Charles E. Roberts House is similar to the spirit of English Arts and Crafts designs,[41] although it is far more geometric and balanced in its massed horizontal and vertical lines. Lack of ornamentation emphasizes the beauty of the fumed oak surface. While machinery was extensively used to make this table, the hand of the

CAT. NO. 25. Kalo Shop
Water Pitcher, 1910
Presented to Preston Owsley on the
occasion of her marriage to Sterling Morton
Inscribed on the base: STERLING / HAND-
BEATEN / AT / KALO SHOPS / PARK RIDGE /
ILLS. / 6863
Silver; 18.4 x 16.5 cm
Gift of Mrs. Eugene A. Davidson, 1973.345

CAT. NO. 26. Frank Lloyd Wright
(1867–1959)
Library Table, 1896
From the Charles E. Roberts House,
Oak Park, Illinois
Manufactured by John W. Ayers, Chicago
Oak and pine; 77.9 x 121.3 cm
Gift of Roger White in memory of Charles
E. Roberts, 1966.389

craftsman is also apparent in the beading. At this early date, Wright was designing his furniture to match the building environment. The Roberts library table is of the same wood and contains the same detailing as the paneled room for which it was intended.[42]

27. Frank Lloyd Wright, *Side Chair,* 1904

The Larkin Administration Building (1903–04; Buffalo) and its furnishings were utilitarian. For the building itself, Wright designed a large, central courtyard lit by a skylight. In this area, employees shared long desks with legless metal chairs attached, which were, in effect, self-contained work stations. Wood furniture, however, was also found throughout the building. The Art Institute's oak side chair was probably used in the employee dining area of the company[43] and is an early expression of Wright's designs that maximized the use of machinery. Simple oak boards were joined in such a manner that their intersecting planes became the design itself.

Wright's inspiration may have been examples by Christopher Dresser published in *Principles of Decora-tive Design* in 1873. In his illustrations for chairs, Dresser showed a slanting backboard joined to a seat frame and commented "that it cannot be doubted that a well-constructed work, however plain or simple it may be, gives satisfaction to those who behold it—while a work of the most elaborate character fails to satisfy if badly constructed."[44]

Uncannily, Wright's chair design for the Larkin Building developed the geometric balance and spatial effects that Charles Rennie Mackintosh also explored in the high-backed oak chairs designed for the Glasgow School of Art the same year. Years later, Wright's early conception of planar, rectilinear seating reached its apogee in Gerrit Rietveld's 1918 classic *Red-Blue Chair* (fig. 10). Wright used the Larkin Building chair, with minor variations, and usually with taller back posts, for other buildings. Other related chairs were designed for Wright's Oak Park studio (1904),[45] Unitarian Church (1904; Oak Park), and Hillside Home School (1903; Spring Green, Wisconsin).

FIGURE 10. Gerrit Rietveld (Dutch, 1888–1964). *Red-Blue Chair,* 1920–21. Painted plywood; 85.7 x 66 x 81.3 cm. The Art Institute of Chicago, Richard T. Crane, Jr., Endowment; through prior gift of Mrs. Albert Beverdge; through prior acquisitions of the funds of Marry Waller Langhorn and through prior acquisition of the R. T. Crane, Jr., Memorial Fund; through prior gift of Florene May Schoenborn and Samuel A. Marx (1988.274).

FACING PAGE: CAT. NO. 27.
Frank Lloyd Wright
Side Chair, 1904
From the Larkin Administration Building,
Employees Dining Area,
Buffalo, New York
Oak; 95.4 x 35.6 x 49.5 cm
Bessie Bennett Fund, 1977.523

CAT. NO. 28. Frank Lloyd Wright
in conjuction with George Mann Neidecken
Desk, 1908
From the Avery Coonley House,
Riverside, Illinois
Oak; 144.9 x 102 x 60.6 cm
Restricted gift of the Graham Foundation
for Advanced Studies in the Fine Arts,
1972.304

28. Frank Lloyd Wright, in conjunction with George
Mann Niedecken, *Desk,* 1908

Wright considered the Avery Coonley House (1908; Riverside, Illinois) to be one of his most successful designs. It
reflected the partnership between a liberal client and great
designer, which was cemented by trust. The Coonleys
were a sophisticated and charming couple; they were progressive thinkers, publicists and practitioners of Christian
Science, and they were drawn to Wright because they
admired his rational planning and "the countenance of
principle."[46] The Coonley House was one of the architect's most completely designed interiors; he designed
everything in the house including the carpets, table service, and linens.[47]

The Art Institute's desk was intended for the rear
guest room of the Coonley House and echoes the facade's
interesting geometric forms and broad cantilever (fig. 11).
Small square doors with decorative banding suggest the
casement windows, and applied horizontal moldings across
the base supports echo those on the exterior of the building.

A watercolor rendering of the desk by interior architect George Mann Niedecken (fig. 12) shows the collaboration between Wright and the president of the interior
design firm of Niedecken-Walbridge Company, Milwaukee.[48] The two probably met through the Arts and
Crafts Society, and Niedecken worked in Wright's studio
in 1904.[49] Scholars disagree about the amount of auton-
omy Niedecken had in designing furniture for Wright's
houses. While Niedecken made finished renderings such
as this one, he probably worked from Wright's sketches.
He may also have finished details of the Coonley House
interior after Wright left for Germany in 1909. Indeed,
the moldings that form the desk's feet are typical of

FIGURE 12. George Mann Niedecken for
Frank Lloyd Wright. *Rendering of a Desk
for the Avery Coonley House*, c. 1907. Ink
and watercolor on paper; 27.9 x 39.4 cm.
The Art Institute of Chicago, Gift of Mr.
and Mrs. James Howlett (1990.41).

FIGURE 11. Frank Lloyd Wright. Avery
Coonley House, Riverside, Illinois, 1908.
Photo: Henry Fuermann.

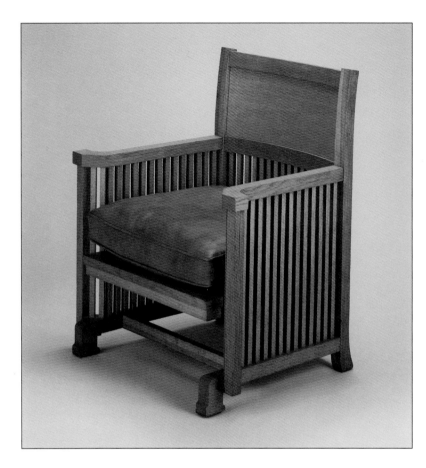

CAT. NO. 29. Frank Lloyd Wright
Armchair, 1908
From the Ray W. Evans House, Chicago
Oak; 86.9 x 58.5 x 57.1 cm
Gift of Mrs. and Mrs. F. M. Fahrenwald,
1970.435

CAT. NO. 30. Frank Lloyd Wright
Desk and Chair, 1939
Manufactured by Steelcase, Inc.
From the S. C. Johnson and Son
Administration Building, Racine,
Wisconsin
Armchair: painted steel tubing, maple
armrests, upholstery; 88.8 x 40.3 x 43.2 cm
Desk: painted steel tubing, maple work sur-
face, with later laminated surface; 72.9 x
213.4 x 81.3 cm
Gift of the Johnson Wax Company,
1972.310–311

Niedecken's designs rather than Wright's simpler conceptions. Niedecken was a capable designer in his own right, designing murals, special fixtures, and furniture.[50] His sympathy for the Prairie School's integration of the building with its furnishings and natural environment made him an ideal choice for collaborations with architects such as Wright, George Grant Elmslie, and George W. Maher.

Niedecken's asymmetrical wash drawing with floating panels in overlapping planes, meandering vine, and flattened decorative elements recalls Japanese prints. The repeated squares of doors, handles, and pottery also echo the influence of the Vienna Secessionist designs of Josef Hoffmann and Koloman Moser.

29. Frank Lloyd Wright, *Armchair*, 1908

Square in plan, the Ray W. Evans House (1908) was built in the Beverly neighborhood on Chicago's South Side, and was another of Wright's integrated Prairie compositions. Wright, who hated radiators, designed radiator covers composed of vertical slats that allowed efficient heat circulation. In keeping with such utilitarian objects, Wright designed chairs and tables that extended the vertical-slat theme. Wright had created massive, square solid-oak armchairs for the B. Harley Bradley House (1900; Kankakee, Illinois), one of which is in the collection of the David and Alfred Smart Museum of Art at the University of Chicago. The Evans armchair is a more sophisticated interpretation of the form, using positive and negative space to lighten the oak mass, and adding the L-shaped foot to strengthen and broaden the chair's presence. This foot treatment, compared to the ball feet of the vertical-slat armchair designed by Purcell, Feick and Elmslie (cat no. 22), gives the chair a monumental presence. Where Purcell, Feick and Elmslie's chair seems tight and self-contained, Wright's armchair seems to expand into the space around it.

The Art Institute also owns a library table from the Evans House that repeats the square, solid-oak mass, penetrated and lightened by vertical elements.

30. Frank Lloyd Wright, *Desk and Chair*, 1939

Although later than Wright's Prairie School experiments, the S. C. Johnson and Son Administration Building (1936; Racine, Wisconsin) was a totally integrated environment. Wright designed practically all the interior elements, the mushroom columns, glass tubing, walls, skylights, heating and lighting systems, and the furniture. As in his earlier Larkin Building (1903–04; Buffalo), Wright designed a large main workroom replete with specialized furniture.

Wright's early design for the furnishings (published in *Architectural Forum* in January 1938) shows that he originally thought about welded, heavy sheet-aluminum components for this project. The tubular-steel version was certainly cheaper to produce and was perhaps suggested by Steelcase, Inc., or Warren McArthur, the two firms that submitted prototypes for the project.[51] Tubular-steel furniture had been designed by Marcel Breuer in 1925, and shortly thereafter by both Ludwig Mies van der Rohe and Le Corbusier.

Wright wanted the furniture, executed in the end by Steelcase, to reflect both the mushroom shape of the columns and the cantilevered quality of the structure itself. The three-legged chairs for the secretarial pool were made of russet-painted steel tubing and matching upholstery. Wright believed that the design would allow employees free movement of their feet and promote better posture.[52] The desks, with swinging undertables for typewriters, were made of tubular steel and maple work surfaces, with a cantilevered shelf to hold files (The worn work surfaces were later laminated with a plastic surface.) A wastebasket is supported by the tubular steel frame.

The desks and chairs are also early expressions of the now-common idea of modular furniture used in open office planning.

PRAIRIE SCHOOL WORKS IN THE RYERSON AND BURNHAM LIBRARIES AT THE ART INSTITUTE OF CHICAGO

MARY WOOLEVER
Architectural Archivist
Ryerson and Burnham Libraries
The Art Institute of Chicago

The collections of Prairie School materials in the Ryerson and Burnham Libraries at The Art Institute of Chicago grew by slow accretion, from myriad sources, and without a focused plan of acquisition. Most archival collections were received as unsolicited donations, and the published materials (excluding periodicals) were purchased in a random fashion or received in the gifts of architects' libraries. Despite this disorderly growth, the libraries are now able to offer a strong research collection, capable of sustaining in-depth scholarly research. The variety of materials is vast, and it includes photographs of Frank Lloyd Wright buildings purchased from the photographer Henry Fuermann; a gift of architectural photographs from Thomas Eddy Tallmadge; archival collections of Louis Sullivan materials donated by George Grant Elmslie, Hugh Morrison, and John B. Van Allen, grandson of a Sullivan client; papers on Wright's Dwight, Illinois, bank given by the First National Bank of Dwight; promotional business brochures of architects such as George W. Maher; and trade catalogues for terracotta, ornamental iron, and concrete companies.

Several factors influenced the growth and nature of the collections documenting the Prairie School. Of greatest importance was the fact that the architects loosely gathered together in the "school" did not develop a publishing mechanism to serve as their proselytizing medium; nor, with the exception of Sullivan and Wright, were they particularly prolific writers, as either historians, critics, or theorists. There was no manifesto of beliefs or a single, unifying treatise; and there was no periodical devoted to the movement that recorded its evolution.

There were, of course, sources in the Art Institute's library that documented the movement: prior to the establishment of the Burnham Library in 1912, the Ryerson Library maintained subscriptions to the architecture journals (for example, *The Inland Architect and News Record, The Architectural Record, The Western Architect,* and *The Brickbuilder*) in which Prairie School projects were presented. These periodicals also published occasional essays by the architects Maher, Robert C. Spencer, Jr., and Tallmadge. Another publishing venue was the catalogue of the annual exhibition of the Chicago Architectural Club, which included numerous works by the Prairie School group at the beginning of the century. Because the exhibitions were held at the Art Institute from 1894 to 1928, the library handily acquired the accompanying catalogues.

The timing of the establishment of the new architecture library was inauspicious for the development of a strong Prairie School collection. At that time, Wright's several trips to Europe had diminished his presence and that of his office in Chicago, and he would leave for Japan in January 1913 to work on the Imperial Hotel in Tokyo. Walter Burley Griffin was announced the win-

FACING PAGE, LEFT: George W. Maher. Photo courtesy of the Kenilworth Historical Society.

FACING PAGE, RIGHT TOP: Thomas E. Tallmadge. Photo by Walinger, courtesy of the Chicago Historical Society (ICHi-23863).

FACING PAGE, RIGHT BOTTOM: Vernon S. Watson.

ner of the competition to design Canberra, Australia's new capital city, and would soon leave the country (with his wife Marion Mahony Griffin), never to return; Purcell and Elmslie had established an active office in Minneapolis; and the remaining Prairie School architects had developed more individualistic expressions of the style that Wright initially codified.

The personalities involved in planning the Burnham Library's collections and services were decidedly not adherents of the Prairie School in sentiment and practice. The first library committee included Hubert Burnham, Peirce Anderson, and Edward H. Bennett (all trained at the Ecole des Beaux-Arts in Paris), and, as chairman, Howard Van Doren Shaw, an architect best known for his eclectic European-inspired residences. To build the collections, the library committee solicited lists of the most valuable and frequently used book titles from East Coast institutions—Columbia University, Cornell University, the Massachusetts Institute of Technology, and the University of Pennsylvania. Locally, they visited the libraries of the architectural firms Holabird and Roche, and Coolidge and Hodgdon, which were known for their commercial and civic buildings. The leading personalities of the Prairie School movement—Wright, the Griffins, Tallmadge (who did become a library committee member in 1928), Watson, William Drummond, and Maher —were not participants in the early development of the library. By 1927, when the Burnham Library committee first solicited contributions of architectural drawings representing the "best architecture of today," the Prairie School had already lost its impact and design force. Instead, drawings were solicited from Cram and Ferguson, Paul Cret, and John Russell Pope.

In the library's development, Sullivan held a preeminent and perhaps unique position among the architects associated with the Prairie School. In 1922 the library committee participated in the commissioning of Sullivan to prepare a set of drawings to illustrate his aesthetic philosophy, which was published in 1924 as *A System of Architectural Ornament According with a Philosophy of Man's Powers* (see cat. no. 4). The first major archival collections of Prairie School material were the gifts of Sullivan papers from Elmslie and Morrison in the early 1930s, which included Sullivan's preliminary drawings for *A System of Architectural Ornament;* manuscripts of *The Autobiography of an Idea* and *Kindergarten Chats;* and photographs and personal memorabilia.

After the Depression, the driving architectural force was modernism, accelerated by the presence of Ludwig Mies van der Rohe as the new director of the School of Architecture at the Armour Institute (now the Illinois Institute of Technology). John Holabird, the chairman of the library committee, thought that the library "should be mainly concerned with serving the current needs of the architects, and let the Newberry Library take care of the historic part with the exception of some of the outstanding authorities of each age."[1]

It was not until after World War II that the staff and the committee came to understand the historical importance of the regional style and began to more aggressively collect papers and drawings documenting Chicago's unique architectural past. This belated attention to the Prairie School was probably inspired by the relatively contemporaneous publications reevaluating the movement, such as Hugh Morrison's *Louis Sullivan: Prophet of Modern Architecture* (1935), Sigfried Giedion's *Space, Time, and Architecture: The Growth of a New Tradition* (1941), and Henry Russell Hitchcock's *In the Nature of Materials, 1887–1941: The Buildings of Frank Lloyd Wright* (1942). These authors conducted research in the collections of the Burnham Library. The library sponsored a major exhibition of Sullivan materials in 1956, followed by exhibitions of Sullivan's *System of Architectural Ornament* drawings, furniture designs of Wright, and drawings by the Griffins. A major body of architectural drawings was borrowed from architectural firms, clients, and heirs in the early 1950s for a microfilming project jointly sponsored by the Burnham Library and the University of Illinois. It included projects by Adler and Sullivan, Louis Sullivan, George Grant Elmslie, the Griffins, Frank Lloyd Wright, Purcell, Feick and Elmslie, and Tallmadge and Watson.[2]

Today, many decades after the zenith of the Prairie School, the opportunity to acquire major collections of architects' or designers' papers has essentially passed. Extant papers of individuals associated with the Prairie School are now primarily in institutional collections, although occasionally there are opportunities to acquire small groups of photographs or discrete collections of correspondence, or a contemporaneous publication not represented in the libraries' holdings. In the past decade, the most significant addition to the libraries' holdings of Prairie School materials has been the archives of the Prairie School Press, a trailblazer in the publication and dissemination of research on the broad spectrum of Prairie School architecture. Donated by the founders Marilyn Whittlesey Hasbrouck and Wilbert R. Hasbrouck, the collection contains published and unpublished manuscripts, research notes, and correspondence with authors and scholars, gathered in the 1960s and 1970s during the publishing years of the press.

The following entries present a sampling of the rich diversity of published materials and archival documents in the libraries' collections.

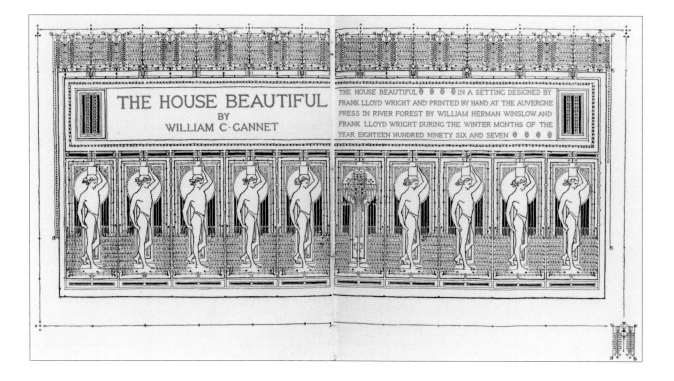

Frank Lloyd Wright

Of the Prairie School architects, Frank Lloyd Wright and his mentor (or "lieber Meister") Louis Sullivan were the most prolific writers, but Wright alone was interested in book design and in the printing process.[3] Very early in his independent practice he joined with two of his architectural clients—William H. Winslow, owner of the Winslow Brothers Company, makers of ornamental iron products, and Chauncey Williams, partner in the publishing firm Way and Williams[4]—to design and print two books under the imprint of the Auvergne Press. The first volume, *The Eve of St. Agnes,* with illustrations by Wright for the poem by John Keats, was published in 1896, and the second, *The House Beautiful* (cat. no. 31), was printed in the winter of 1896–97.[5]

To the text of *The House Beautiful,* based on a sermon by the Unitarian minister William C. Gannett,[6] Wright added a double-page title printed with red text and black ornamentation; a repeated full-page pattern in black lines for the thirteen divider pages; and an individualized design, again in black ink, surrounding the text for each of the six chapters. The beginning of each chapter is emphasized by an ornamental tailpiece with the chapter title, both of which were printed in red. According to his son John Lloyd, Wright "designed the setting and drew the intricate pattern freehand with pen and ink."[7]

The book's design was first extensively discussed in

CAT. NO. 31. Frank Lloyd Wright
(1867–1959), designer and printer
The House Beautiful, title pages
Text by William C. Gannett
River Forest, Ill.: Auvergne Press, 1896–97

Robert C. Spencer, Jr.'s article "The Work of Frank Lloyd Wright" in *The Architectural Review* (June 1900). In the twelve-page article, five illustrations are devoted to details from the page decorations. Spencer wrote of these patterns: "See how beautifully these schemes are built up and knit together, how intelligently surface and void, mass and line are contrasted, blended and harmonized, how major and minor accents are introduced and disposed for the most pleasing repetition. In the matter of technique the composition of this ornament is identical with that of musical composition at its best . . . in which line and color, instead of the qualities of tone are the media of expression."[8] In a poetic statement after the title page, Wright suggested a non-musical metaphor: "With nature-warp of naked weed by printer-craft imprisoned, we weave this interlinear web. / A rythmic [sic] changing play of ordered space and image seeking trace our fabric makes, / to clothe with chastity and grace our author's gentle word. Appreciation of the beauty / in his work we weave,—in part ourselves to please, yet may we better fare, and, weaving so, with you our pleasure share."

Both music and textile images are needed to aptly describe the linear pattern of parallel lines and dots suggesting musical notation, as well as the intricately intertwined pattern of curved lines that appear like woven reeds.[9]

It is ironic but revealing that the most important contemporaneous publications documenting Wright's prairie years were published in Europe: *Ausgeführte Bauten und Entwürfe von Frank Lloyd Wright,* published in Berlin by Ernst Wasmuth in 1911 and commonly known as the "Wasmuth portfolio,"[10] and the seven issues of the Dutch arts periodical *Wendingen* published in 1925. The *Ausgeführte Bauten* was published as a two-portfolio compendium of architectural drawings spanning Wright's career in private practice, beginning with the Winslow House of 1893 in River Forest, Illinois. The seventy-two lithographic plates, measuring 16" x 25¼" (40.5 x 64.4 cm), were printed on either ivory or gray paper, in gray or brown ink; two prints were given a heightened style with bronze powder.[11] The unique Unity Temple drawing (cat. no. 32) was printed in gray, green, and brown tones in addition to the brown ink used for lines. Additional plans, details, or elevations were printed on tissue overlays attached to twenty-six plates.

Wright contracted with the Wasmuth company for 1,275 copies of the portfolios, including twenty-five copies of a deluxe edition "printed on Japan paper and bound in half-leather" for Wright's personal use.[12] With assistance from several clients—Charles E. Roberts, Francis W. Little, and Darwin D. Martin—Wright had financed the print run, expecting to recover the investment from the profits of sales in the United States; however, he failed to find book dealers to sell the portfolios, and had to advertise them himself in mail-order fashion.[13] The majority of these copies were stored at Taliesin and were lost in the fire of 1914.

In 1925 the second important survey of Wright's Prairie School projects appeared in Europe in the Dutch periodical *Wendingen* (cat. no. 33), which published illustrations of projects and reprinted numerous articles by

CAT. NO. 32. Frank Lloyd Wright, architect
"Unity Temple," plate LXIV
*Ausgeführte Bauten und Entwürfe
von Frank Lloyd Wright*
Berlin: Ernst Wasmuth, 1911

THE LIFE-WORK OF THE AMERICAN ARCHITECT FRANK LLOYD WRIGHT WITH CONTRIBUTIONS BY FRANK LLOYD WRIGHT ■ AN INTRODUCTION BY ARCHITECT H. TH. WIJDEVELD AND MANY ARTICLES BY FAMOUS EUROPEAN ARCHITECTS AND AMERICAN WRITERS ■ PUBLISHER: C. A. MEES SANTPOORT HOLLAND ■1925

CAT. NO. 33. "The Life-work of the American Architect Frank Lloyd Wright," cover illustration *Wendingen,* 1925

Wright and about Wright by such authors as Hendrik Petrus Berlage, Erich Mendelsohn, Louis Sullivan, and Lewis Mumford.[14] *Wendingen,* founded by the Dutch architect and designer Hendrikus Theodorus Wijdeveld in 1918, appealed to a broad spectrum of design professionals, with issues dedicated to architecture, applied arts, sculpture, painting and graphics, theater and dance.[15] Other non-Dutch architects and artists surveyed were Lyonel Feininger, Gustav Klimt, Diego Rivera, Eileen Gray, Josef Hoffmann, and Erich Mendelsohn.

The selection of projects included a few renderings and plans first published in the Wasmuth portfolio, such as drawings for the Coonley House, McCormick House, and Unity Temple. Unlike the Wasmuth publication, photographs of the finished projects were added, plus several views of building models. Naturally, Wright included more recent work—Taliesin, Midway Gardens, Hollyhock House for Aline Barnsdall, Tokyo's Imperial Hotel and other projects in Japan, and the A. D. German Warehouse in Richland Center, Wisconsin—designed in the fourteen years since the 1911 publication of the Wasmuth portfolio.

While Wright had completed several important projects during the period from 1911 to 1925, his critical success was nominal, although the American press was enthralled with the Imperial Hotel, especially its survival of the 1923 earthquake. Wright himself experienced per-

sonal tragedy at this time: the murder of his companion Mamah Borthwick Cheney, his divorce from Catherine Wright, and the fire at Taliesin. These personal calamities made the timing of the *Wendingen* publication particularly important to Wright, and he was grateful for its publication throughout the rest of his career. In her introduction to the 1965 Horizon Press edition, Olgivanna Lloyd Wright wrote, "Mr. Wright kept this Wendingen edition close by his side. . . . This book was always there [in his room]. . . . I believe the book often served as a relaxation for him to look through. . . . He admired its proportions and layout, and enjoyed turning the pages over. . . . To him this was the book on architecture that would be good a hundred years from now; he believed it would have as much impact on the future as it has already had on the past."[16]

Marion Mahony Griffin's "Magic of America"

One of the rarities in the Ryerson and Burnham Libraries is the unpublished typescript "The Magic of America" by Marion Mahony Griffin.[17] The typescript, over 1,000 pages in length with handwritten annotations and nearly 200 illustrations, narrates, in nonchronological and unrelated brief essays, the biography of her husband Walter Burley Griffin and her own autobiography (see the essay

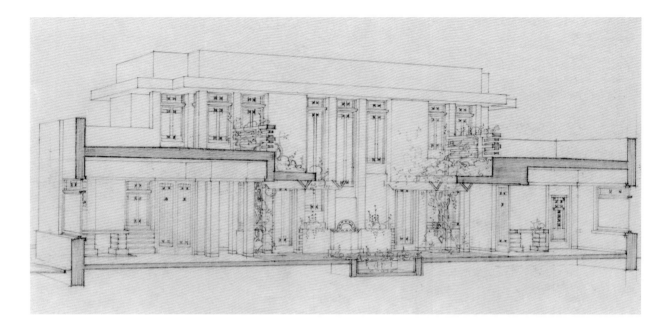

by Janice Pregliasco in this issue, pp. 164–81, for a more complete discussion of the Griffins). As early as 1940, Marion hoped to publish "The Magic of America," which she probably began after Walter's death in 1937.[18] But she was unable to find funding to do so, and she donated the documents to the Art Institute in 1949.

Marion drew upon numerous sources for her text: letters between her husband and herself, and correspondence with family, friends, and business colleagues; Walter's writings and lectures; and other published sources. To illustrate the text she collected photographs, blueprints, newspaper and magazine articles, brochures, and some original sketches (see cat. no. 34, which is identified as the Graham Dwelling, Melbourne, on the print in the New-York Historical Society's version of "The Magic of America").

The title "The Magic of America" indicates the couple's idealistic belief in the democratic system that supports and encourages the freedom of the individual: "Only in America has [democracy] been experienced. In democracy the Spirit of the human is released."[19] Significantly, the titles of the four sections of the book—"The Empirial [sic] Battle," "The Federal Battle," "The Municipal Battle," and "The Individual Battle"—suggest that Marion and Walter had many experiences in which democracy was lacking.[20]

The four sections are organized thematically, in a rather confused chronological sequence. The first section, "The Empirial Battle," records the years 1935–37, the years Walter spent in India immediately before his death. During these years he observed India's political struggle against English colonial rule. The second section, "The

Federal Battle," begins with the Griffins winning the international design competition for Canberra, Australia's new federal capital. Initially believing Australia to hold great promise in social and political democracy, Marion recorded here their loss of innocence in their new home. She described numerous occasions of "ruthless" and "all-powerful" bureaucracy in her narration of their experiences in city planning projects.[21] Castlecrag, a new suburb of Sydney, is one of the themes of the third section, "The Municipal Battle." In their designs for this suburb, developed between 1920 and 1935, the Griffins distilled their expectations and goals for society. Describing the design, site planning, and construction of individual buildings, Marion highlighted their battles with banks, city officials, and building owners. The last section, "The Individual Battle," contains many references to the personal story of the Griffins; sometimes Marion referred to her husband and herself as Socrates and his wife, Xanthippe, to contrast the self-assuredness of Socrates and the quick temper of Xanthippe. This was the battle of two distinctive personalities struggling to build both a personal and a professional relationship, a battle Marion thought necessary. "I myself . . . have said that it was absurd to look upon the marital relationship, if it were based on love, as having any relation to friendship, that it was more like that of enemies . . . one should not choose a mate as a friend but as an opponent, an opportunity worthy of her mettle."[22]

In this wide-ranging work, Marion repeatedly underscored several themes: the importance of the relationship between architecture and planning in Walter's work; the inspiration both architects derived from Louis

CAT. NO. 34. Walter Burley Griffin
(1876–1937)
"Dwelling—Interior Court" (Graham
Dwelling, Melbourne), c. 1915
Graphite on paper

CAT. NO. 35. George W. Maher (1864–1926)
"Residence ('Pleasant Home') of John
Farson, Oak Park, Illinois"
*Work of George W. Maher / Architect /
Chicago,* plate 11
Chicago: Wallace Press, c. 1910

CAT. NO. 36. Tallmadge and Watson
"A Modest Suburban Residence with
Excellent Lines"
Modern American Homes, plate 15
H. V. von Holst, editor
Chicago: American School of
Correspondence, 1912

RESIDENCE "PLEASANT HOME" OF JOHN FARSON
OAK PARK, ILLINOIS

GEORGE W. MAHER, ARCHITECT
CHICAGO

Frame and Plaster Residence of Remarkably Low Cost

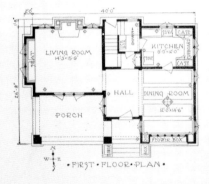

·FIRST·FLOOR·PLAN·

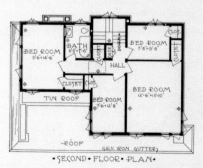

·SECOND·FLOOR·PLAN·

A Modest Suburban Residence with Excellent Lines

*Tallmadge & Watson, Architects,
Chicago, Illinois*

THIS residence, which is the home of Mr. Gustavus Babson, Oak Park, Illinois, is a successful attempt on the part of the architects to solve the problem of the high cost of building. Its architecture was determined entirely by considerations of economy both in the materials used and in the method of putting them together, regardless of precedent. The rough character of the material harmonizes with the strong design. Narrow boarding is used on the lower part, while the panels in the second story are of pebbled roofing felt which resembles plaster. The interior trim is plain birch. The house was built in 1906 at a cost of $4,600.

·NORTH·ELEVATION·

PLATE 15

Sullivan's work; her denigration of the achievements of Frank Lloyd Wright; and, in the broadest social arena, the importance of fighting for individual freedom.

George W. Maher

Like Frank Lloyd Wright, George Washington Maher (1864–1926) apprenticed in the office of Chicago architect Joseph Lyman Silsbee, and encouraged the development of an indigenous American architecture; but, as the illustration from a 1910 brochure reveals (cat. no. 35), Maher's designs developed in an idiosyncratic, non-Wrightian expression of the Prairie School.

Maher left Silsbee's office in 1888 to open his independent practice, primarily as a sole practitioner until he was joined by his son Philip after World War I. The majority of Maher's projects were residences for Chicago-area businessmen, such as John Farson (1897; Oak Park; see cat. no. 35, and the article by Judith A. Barter in this issue, pp. 116–18), James Patten (1903; Evanston), and Harry Rubens (1903; Glencoe).

With the Farson House, Maher expressed his maturing sensibilities, moving away from the picturesque gables and turrets and asymmetry of Silsbee's Shingle Style, and toward strong, symmetrical massing, a relatively horizontal emphasis, and a prominent central entrance. Maher's buildings lack the sweep of Wright's best designs, and they do not display the inside-outside interplay of spaces using terraces, porches, and long bands of windows that characterized Wright's work. As the architectural historian David Gebhard said, Maher produced a "monumental Prairie School architecture" with "classic solidity."[23]

The illustration of the Farson House is drawn from a brochure privately published around 1910 by Maher, which he inscribed "My compliments to Mr. Henry Hill. 1910" and signed. Such "vanity" publications, which were probably used to attract more business, were one of the few means of promoting the architect's projects and client base because paid advertising was not permitted by the American Institute of Architects.[24]

The single-page preface to this brochure and a similar one in the Ryerson and Burnham Libraries succinctly presented Maher's theory of design: "The architect should grasp all opportunities and adhering strictly to the requirements of the situation, harmonize all inspiration into his work." In several articles written for *The Western Architect* and *The Architectural Record*, Maher elaborated on his philosophy that the architect should free himself from the confining strictures of historical precedent and look at each new commission with fresh inspiration. He wrote that architects must "dip deep into the currents of life around about us, feel the pulse of the times and then

actually execute the ideals of the present hour, and if we do this work truthfully, intelligently, our efforts must be enduring."[25]

Hermann von Holst

In the first sentence of his preface to *Modern American Homes,* published in 1912 by the American School of Correspondence in Chicago, Hermann Valentin von Holst (1874–1955) clearly stated the impetus for the book: "The American home has undergone many changes in the last twenty years." He identified the particular importance of the residential movement out of central city apartment buildings to single-family residences in suburban settings. Along with this change came improvements in construction techniques, higher standards of sanitation, and affordable levels of comfort. His goal was to further stimulate and direct "this increasing appreciation of good building and of comfortable country homes on the part of city people."[26]

In 108 plates, von Holst presented an array of contemporary dwellings, most built in the five-year period preceding the 1912 publication date (see cat. no. 36). One hundred of the plates illustrate single-family residences, and the remainder document small apartment buildings and civic buildings. They are variously described as artistic or inexpensive bungalows, cottages, country homes, colonial residences, and compact homes for small cities. Floor plans accompany virtually all exterior photographs of the homes, and occasionally a site plan or interior view is included.

In his numerous editorial comments, von Holst sought to develop a sense of taste and quality in his readers, encouraging them to pursue fine buildings within reasonable budgets. He commented on the arrangements of rooms, and the selection of appropriate materials based on their cost and durability. The construction cost of virtually all of the illustrated residences was published, often with notes on construction methods, and von Holst suggested cost-effective choices that were also aesthetically pleasing.

While important Prairie School architects represented in the book included Walter Burley Griffin, Tallmadge and Watson, Spencer and Powers, George W. Maher, William Purcell, and Frank Lloyd Wright, the book was not solely devoted to that style. It offered a broad range of stylistic expressions, from modest California bungalows to "colonial farmhouses," by a national group of architects.

The intention of *Modern American Homes* was essentially didactic. Its publisher, the American School of Correspondence, offered, as its name suggests, home-study courses for professional and personal self-improvement. The school's curriculum for its architecture programs

CAT. NO. 37. Alfred S. Alschuler (1876–1940)
Hump Hairpin Manufacturing
Company Building
Common Clay (July 1920), pages iv–v

appealed to a large nationwide audience of architects, builders, and potential homeowners.[27]

Von Holst's own architectural practice was relatively undistinguished and nearly as eclectic as the styles represented in *Modern American Homes.* He served as an associate professor of architecture at the Armour Institute of Architecture in 1905–06, and he designed a number of Commonwealth Edison substations in the 1910s and 1920s. Von Holst produced several other publications for the American School of Correspondence, which were more focused on the Beaux-Arts aesthetic. One of his most notable and notorious achievements was managing Frank Lloyd Wright's office while Wright was in Europe completing *Ausgeführte Bauten und Entwürfe von Frank*

Lloyd Wright (see cat. no. 32), during which time he employed Marion Mahony and Walter Burley Griffin. The business arrangement with Wright ended in an acrimonious dispute concerning the division of fees and clients, which may partly explain von Holst's inclusion of only a single plate illustrating Wright's projects in *Modern American Homes.*[28]

Building Materials and Trade Catalogues

The ornamental uses of terracotta (Latin for burned earth) are primarily associated with the work of Louis Sullivan, and Purcell and Elmslie. The sculptural decoration of their buildings is iconic in the study of Prairie School architecture. On the other hand, the uses of concrete as a decorative and structural material are less well known. Two trade publications, one representing each material, sugguest a wealth of research sources on the Prairie School.

In response to the devastation of the Chicago Fire of 1871, the building trades quickly adopted terracotta, previously produced for drainpipes and flowerpots, for its ready availability, its low cost, and its lightweight fireproof qualities.[29] On building exteriors, terracotta pieces were used in imitation of stone for lintels, sills, string courses, and arches on brick and stone buildings after the fire (in, for example, the Dearborn Street Station of 1885); and in the 1890s terracotta appeared as glazed and often decoratively ornamented "tiles" for exterior cladding (as in the Reliance Building of 1894).[30]

Hollow tiles were used to sheath the metal members of the new skyscrapers' structural skeletons and to fill wall and floor cavities. Coincidentally, Sullivan began to explore the plasticity of terracotta, finding it an expressive medium for his three-dimensional statements of nat-

ural, organic pattern (as in the Wainwright Building in St. Louis of 1890, the Guaranty Building in Buffalo of 1894, and the facade of the Gage Building in Chicago of 1898).[31] Besides the major commercial structures in the Chicago Loop, countless one- and two-story commercial buildings throughout the city featured terracotta ornament. Most were of brick with terracotta ornament supplied by the major companies in Chicago: Chicago Terra Cotta Company (founded in 1868), Northwestern Terra Cotta Works (founded in 1877), American Terra Cotta and Ceramic Company (founded in 1881), and Midland Terra Cotta Company (founded in 1910).[32]

In addition to catalogues, several companies produced periodicals illustrating buildings with terracotta

CAT. NO. 38. Frank Lloyd Wright
Midway Gardens (details)
Beauty and Utility in Concrete, pages 16–17
Chicago: Chicago Portland Cement
Company, c. 1914

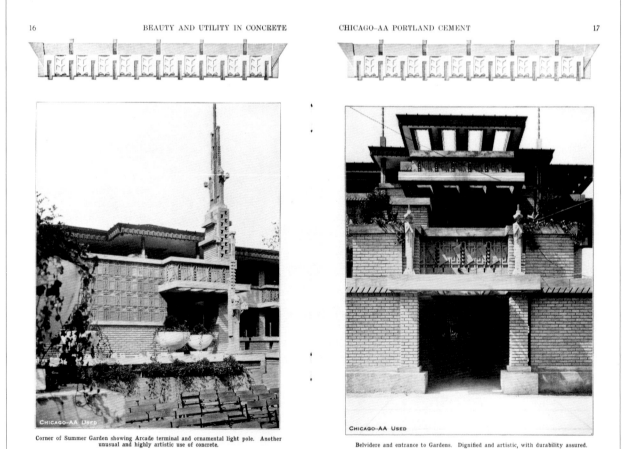

16   BEAUTY AND UTILITY IN CONCRETE   CHICAGO-AA PORTLAND CEMENT   17

CHICAGO–AA USED

Corner of Summer Garden showing Arcade terminal and ornamental light pole. Another unusual and highly artistic use of concrete.

CHICAGO–AA USED

Belvidere and entrance to Gardens. Dignified and artistic, with durability assured.

ornament that were meant to inspire greater use of their products. The first issue of *Common Clay* (cat. no. 37), published in 1920 by the American Terra Cotta and Ceramic Company, featured the Hump Hairpin Manufacturing Company Building by Alfred S. Alschuler (1876–1940).[33] This one-story brick commercial building (at the corner of Prairie Avenue and 20th Street, quite near the terracotta company offices at Prairie and 18th) expressed the last vestiges of a commercial style of Prairie School design: a strong horizontality through flush vertical mortar joints and deeply raked horizontal joints; a monolithic masonry wall with broad, strong piers separating the recessed windows; modest highlights of ivory-colored, glazed terracotta ornament in simplified geometric shapes without historic design precedent. While Alschuler is not considered a Prairie School architect—he designed very few residences and is best known for the London Guarantee and Accident Building in Chicago—in the 1910s and 1920s he designed numerous small commercial buildings for the industrial periphery of downtown Chicago.[34]

Published sporadically for four years, the last issue of *Common Clay* appeared in December 1923, with a frontispiece entitled "The Christmas Spirit of Joy" drawn for the magazine by Sullivan. *Common Clay* was a forum that was intended to encourage the creative use of terracotta by publishing the projects of numerous clients such as Louis Sullivan, Jarvis Hunt, and Frost and Granger, and by offering technical solutions to design and installation problems.

In the first decade of the twentieth century, the cost of concrete had decreased sufficiently to make it a cost-effective construction material. To encourage its use, the Chicago Portland Cement Company produced the brochure *Beauty and Utility in Concrete* (cat. no. 38) celebrating the use of concrete in Frank Lloyd Wright's Midway Gardens, completed in 1914. The brochure's text, drawn from an unidentified article published in *The Cement Era*, offered little commentary on the structural use of concrete. Instead, the text and the sixteen black-and-white illustrations highlight the "artistic possibilities" of the material.[35] Many of the photographs offer close-up views of the sculptural program, which included hundreds of relief panels, nearly one hundred "spindle" (or sprite) figures and the "Queen of the Gardens" figure modeled by Alfonso Iannelli. The published comments praise the successful casting of the figures, some of which required molds of over eighty individual parts. Concrete was not unfamiliar to Wright—even before the construction of Unity Temple of poured concrete (completed in 1908; Oak Park, Illinois) he had designed a pavilion for the Universal Portland Cement Company at the 1901 Pan American Exposition in Buffalo, a residence-studio for

the sculptor Richard Bock in 1908, and a "Fireproof House" (published in *Ladies Home Journal* in April 1907).

As improvements in the production of concrete made it more affordable, its desirable qualities of fireproofing and indestructibility were reinforced by the devastating earthquake and fires of San Francisco in 1906.[36] Concrete eventually joined the machine-age materials of glass and steel to dominate the building technology of the twentieth century, while terracotta virtually disappeared after the era of the flamboyant Art Deco skyscrapers.

Teco and Kalo Wares

The Teco ceramic lines and the handcrafted metalwork from the Kalo Shop embody the simplicity of line and reduced ornament in combination with functional utility that was so prized by the Prairie School architects. Teco and Kalo wares graced many Prairie School interiors, including those of Frank Lloyd Wright. Early in the twentieth century both companies, which were based in the Chicago metropolitan area, established a reputation for finely designed and executed wares.

Teco (adapted from the word "terracotta") was a decorative housewares line of vases, jardinieres, pitchers, mugs, and other objects, developed by William Day Gates at the Gates Potteries in the late 1890s.[37] Gates also owned the American Terra Cotta and Ceramic Company, which was located across the road in Terra Cotta, Illinois (near present-day Crystal Lake). To appeal to a broad clientele, the price range ran the gamut from a fifty-cent vase to a $65.00 lamp with a Teco vase base and a leaded-glass shade designed by Orlando Giannini. Some eighty pieces were illustrated in the 1905 catalogue *Hints for Gifts and Home Decoration* (cat. no. 39); however, design code numbers in the 300's suggest a much larger production. The outcome of Gates's commitment "to produce an art ware that would harmonize with all its surroundings . . . while adding to the beauty of the flower or leaf placed in the vase"[38] was the popular moss-green mat glaze of Teco, which did indeed harmonize with the natural wood tones of Prairie School interiors.

While Gates designed perhaps half of the items, he also commissioned designs from a number of Chicago-area architects, including William K. Fellows, Hugh M. G. Garden, William LeBaron Jenney, William B. Mundie, George C. Nimmons, and Wright, men Gates met through his association with the Chicago Architectural Club. Gates's association with the club was long-standing: he was an associate member until 1915, when he became an honorary member; and nearly every year the firm purchased an advertisement in the annual exhibition catalogue or served as "patron" for the exhibition. As early as 1894, the American Terra Cotta and Ceramic Company

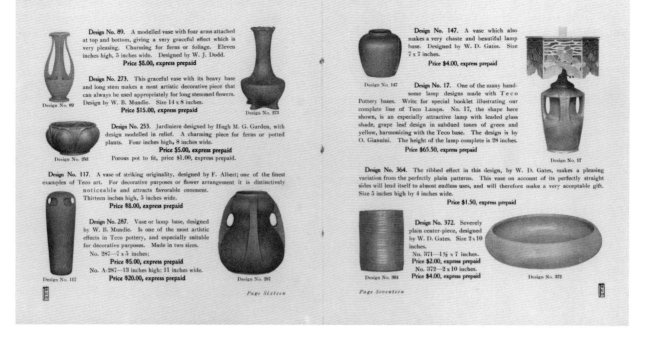

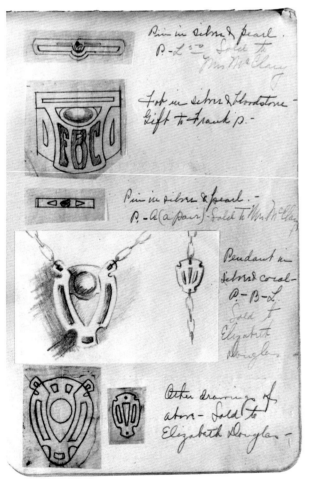

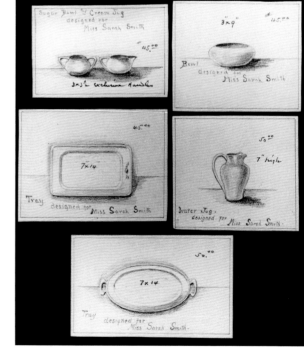

exhibited a vase (which actually predated the introduction of the Teco line); the "exhibit of art pottery" noted in the 1900 catalogue probably consisted of selections of Teco. Teco wares were included in the club's annual exhibition almost every year between 1904 and 1911.

The strongly architectonic profiles of the wares reflect the architectural grounding of many of the designers. Thomas Eddy Tallmadge made an oblique reference to the relationship between Teco pottery and the Prairie School architects in his April 1908 article "The 'Chicago School'": "In the realm of pottery Chicago architects have delved deep, and have encouraged by their demands and their designs the local development of the craft."[39] Gates was in philosophical alignment with Prairie School architects in his desire to produce an American pottery that reflected national values and repudiated the influences of European tradition.

A second source of adornment of the Prairie interior was the metalwork of the Kalo Art-Craft Community, established in Park Ridge in 1905 by Clara Barck Welles and George S. Welles, to produce jewelry and fine metalwork. (See the article by Judith A. Barter in this issue, pp. 125–26, for an extended description.)[40] The Ryerson and Burnham Libraries have a notebook of sketches by Mildred Belle Bevis that represents the individual designer/craftsman of the Kalo community. According to her son Marshall B. Hanks, donor of the sketchbook in 1980, Bevis came from St. Louis to train at the Kalo Shop and later became the first teacher in the silversmithing school. Although the Art Institute does not own any pieces by her, the sketchbook provides a survey of designs, materials, costs, and sizes, with customers' names in many cases. It contains forty-one pages, with small pencil or ink sketches on pieces of onionskin paper that were pasted on the notebook pages (cat. no. 40). Most designs for cuff buttons, watch fobs, pendants, and so on, were to be executed in hammered silver; a few items were available in gold or copper, such as the "top of hand bag in copper." Bevis prepared only a few designs for hollowware or trays; of particular beauty are

CAT. NO. 39. *Hints for Gift and Home Decoration*, pages 16–17
Terra Cotta, Ill: Gates Potteries, 1905

CAT. NO. 40. Mildred Belle Bevis
Designs for jewelry (left);
Five designs for tableware for
Miss Sarah Smith (right)
From notebook of designs for the
Kalo Shop, n.d.
Pencil on paper

the five drawings for custom designs for Miss Sarah Smith, which have the characteristic clarity of line and form, and the minimal ornamentation, for which Kalo wares are renowned.

Roycroft Industries and Craftsman Workshops

In contrast to the architect-dominated Prairie School movement, the broader Arts and Crafts movement in America encompassed a number of publishing businesses offering "little" magazines, catalogues, philosophical treatises, journals, and books. Two of the most prolific publishers/authors/critics were Elbert Hubbard (1856–1915) and Gustav Stickley (1858–1942). Although business competitors, both men shared many features: both were midwesterners who established their businesses in upstate New York; both maintained important publishing activities while also producing furniture and other decorative items for the home; and, perhaps most importantly, both held a vision of improving middle-class taste in America by promoting the aesthetic philosophy of the British designer William Morris (1834–1896) and developing an indigenous American style based on that philosophy.

Hubbard's Roycrofters and Stickley's Craftsman Workshops attained their highest level of commercial success and greatest impact in the first fifteen years of the twentieth century, coinciding with the rise of the Prairie School style. At this same time, the number of urban middle-class Americans able to afford single-family residences was increasing dramatically. Hubbard and Stickley sought to indoctrinate this group with the ideals of William Morris: "Have nothing in your houses that you do not know to be useful, or believe to be beautiful."[41]

Hubbard came to the movement after having made a modest fortune as a very successful salesman and partner in the Larkin Soap Company.[42] In his late thirties he sold his share of the business, briefly enrolled in Harvard University, and in 1893 sailed for Europe to visit the homes of great literary figures, responding most empathetically to the work coming from Morris's Kelmscott Press. Hubbard's European visits inspired his writing of the "Little Journeys" series, introduced by G. P. Putnam's Sons in 1895. Hubbard took over the printing of the series in 1900, producing it at his Roycroft Press.[43] The first volume of *Little Journeys to the Homes of English Authors* (cat. no. 41), a volume devoted to William Morris, was one of the first printed by Hubbard and the Roycrofters in January 1900. The Art Institute's copy, a gift of Laura Welch in 1924, is one of the 925 copies produced in the deluxe edition, bound in a suede soft cover with silk paste-downs.[44]

Until 1915, when Hubbard and his wife died in the sinking of the Lusitania, the press produced "little jour-

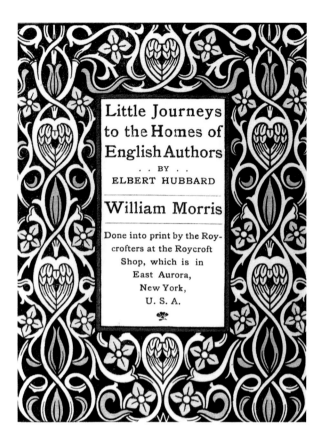

CAT. NO. 41. Elbert Hubbard
William Morris, title page
From the series *Little Journeys to the
Homes of English Authors*
East Aurora, N.Y.: Roycroft Shop, 1900

neys" to the homes of "great musicians," "eminent artists," "eminent orators," "great philosophers," "great scientists," "great lovers," "great reformers," "famous women," "great teachers," and ultimately "great businessmen" in 1909, signaling the change in Hubbard's focus from communal craft colony to savvy business practice. Despite the addition of furniture and decorative lines in 1900, the press and fine-binding studio were most important to Hubbard, and they are one of his more prominent and lasting contributions to the reestablishment of fine printing in America.[45]

Unlike Hubbard, Stickley developed a line of furniture and other household items before entering the world of publishing. But like Hubbard, he had been inspired by William Morris. In the first issue of his periodical, *The Craftsman* (October 1901), which was devoted to Morris, Stickley wrote:

The United Crafts endeavor to promote and to extend the principles established by Morris, in both the artistic and the socialistic sense. In the interests of art, they seek to substitute the luxury of taste for the luxury of costliness; to teach that beauty does not imply elaboration or ornament; to employ only those forms and materials which make for simplicity, individuality and dignity of effect.[46]

In *The Craftsman,* which was published monthly through 1916, Stickley preached a holistic design approach to the single-family residence. He published over 200 plans for residences, illustrated examples of properly furnished rooms, described their desirable features, and published "how-to" instructions on weaving and building furniture. The October 1905 issue initiated a series of articles investigating each room of the house and prescribing its furniture and finishings. In the illustrated essay "The Living Room, Its Many Uses and Its Possibilities for Comfort and Beauty" (cat. no. 42), the author wrote that a room's "charm and individuality spring from its fitness to meet the needs of its occupants as simply and directly as possible, regardless of custom or convention; to express honestly the life that goes on in the house and the character of the people who live in it."[47]

Stickley championed the importance of developing a national, indigenous style of American art "express[ing] the spirit of the American people rather than a superficial quickness and cleverness in the imitation or adaptation of foreign ideas and forms."[48] This emphatic belief in the value of "American-ness" attracted Stickley to the writings of the Chicago architect Louis Sullivan, whose essay "What is Architecture? A Study of the American People of Today" he published in *The Craftsman* in 1906 (cat. no. 43).[49] As the historian Robert C. Twombly pointed out, this essay is Sullivan's "last major theoretical work,"

A CRAFTSMAN LIVING ROOM, SHOWING RECESSED WINDOW SEAT

CAT. NO. 42. "A Craftsman Living Room,
Showing Recessed Window Seat"
The Craftsman
Volume 9, number 1 (October 1905),
page 67

CAT. NO. 43. *The Craftsman,* front cover
Volume 10, number 2 (May 1906)

CAT. NO. 44. David T. Van Zanten, editor
Walter Burley Griffin: Selected Designs
Palos Park, Ill.:
Prairie School Press, 1970

CAT. NO. 45. "George W. Maher"
The Prairie School Review
Volume 1, number 1 (first quarter, 1964)

CAT. NO. 46. *The Architecture
of Purcell and Elmslie*
A reissue of three essays published in
The Western Architect, 1913–15
Park Forest, Ill.:
Prairie School Press, 1965

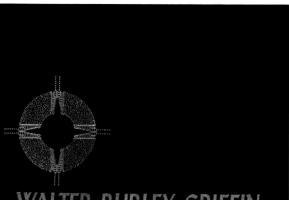

excluding the important late books *The Autobiography of an Idea* (1924), *A System of Architectural Ornament* (1924; see cat. no. 4), and the posthumously published *Democracy: A Man-Search* (1961).[50] In the essay, Sullivan pleaded for the design of buildings that are "modest, truthful and sincere"[51] because the integrity of the architecture is reflected in the people, and vice versa: "You and your architecture are the same. Each is the faithful portrait of the other."[52]

The Prairie School Press

In 1992 Wilbert R. Hasbrouck and Marilyn Whittlesey Hasbrouck donated the archives of the Prairie School Press, which they had founded in 1961 to publish important but out-of-print architecture sources, to the Ryerson and Burnham Libraries. The archives contain published and unpublished manuscripts, correspondence with authors, photographs, and research notes, documenting the twenty-year history of the press. Although neither had a background in publishing or journalism, both Hasbroucks have well-established roots in the Chicago architecture community. Mr. Hasbrouck, a registered architect, was executive director of the Chicago Chapter of the American Institute of Architects from 1968 to 1975, and a founding member and past president of the Chicago Architecture Foundation. In private practice, his firm's work on the restoration of Frank Lloyd Wright's Dana House and Burnham and Root's Rookery Building is well known. Mrs. Hasbrouck's business—the Prairie Avenue Bookshop—has long served scholars, students, and architecture buffs alike.

The first publication of the press was a facsimile edition of Louis Sullivan's *A System of Architectural Ornament According with a Philosophy of Man's Powers,* originally published by the American Institute of Architects in 1924, and the second was a facsimile edition of *The House Beautiful* (see cat. no. 31), published in 1961 and 1963, respectively. In 1965 they reprinted *The Work of Purcell and Elmslie, Architects,* drawn from three articles first published in *The Western Architect* in 1913–15, with a new introduction by David Gebhard (cat. no. 46).[53] New titles published by the press also reflected the Prairie School focus as well as a broader interest in preservation topics: *Historic American Buildings Survey: Chicago and Nearby Illinois Areas* (1966); and *Walter Burley Griffin: Selected Designs* (1970), edited by David T. Van Zanten (cat. no. 44).

The Prairie School Review, first published as a quarterly journal in 1964, was the Hasbroucks' response to the growing number of people interested in the Prairie School. The first issue (cat. no. 45) featured an essay on George W. Maher, with excerpts from Maher's 1887 essay "Originality in American Architecture" (originally published in the October 1887 issue of *The Inland Architect and News Record*), and a selected list of completed structures. Because few of Maher's projects and none of his writings had been published since his death in 1926, this issue provided an exceptional survey of the architect's life and work. The first issue also featured book reviews and news of preservation activities. The essays were well illustrated with photographs and measured drawings. By the third issue, a bibliography had been added, thus setting the essential format of *The Prairie School Review* until its last issue in 1981. The reputations of other architects, similarly forgotten, were rejuvenated: Barry Byrne, Parker Noble Berry, Spencer and Powers, Harvey Ellis, Henry Trost, John Van Bergen, and E. E. Roberts. The *Review* examined the roots of the movement, looking at Sullivan and Joseph Lyman Silsbee; and it explored the Prairie School's influence, such as on the organic architecture of Bruce Goff. In 1972 the Hasbroucks devoted two issues to the symposium "The Chicago School of Architecture," held at Northwestern University in 1969, printing papers by Carl Condit and Winston Weisman, with comments by the panelists Sir John Summerson, Henry Russell Hitchcock, and H. Allen Brooks.

In the last issue, published in 1981, the editors commented on the increasing numbers of books, articles, and exhibitions focused on the Prairie School and related subjects. The Prairie School Press was instrumental in the renaissance of scholarly and public interest in Prairie School architecture and provided a unique publishing forum for a more wide-ranging exploration of the architects and designers working in the style.

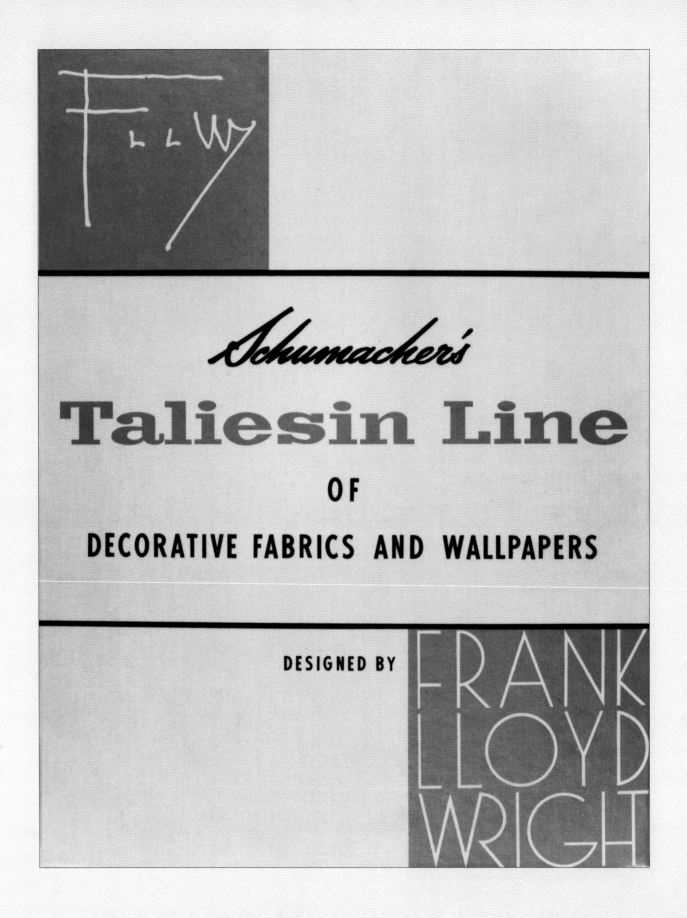

Schumacher's

Taliesin Line

OF

DECORATIVE FABRICS AND WALLPAPERS

DESIGNED BY FRANK LLOYD WRIGH

"MAKE DESIGNS TO YOUR HEART'S CONTENT": THE FRANK LLOYD WRIGHT/SCHUMACHER VENTURE

CHRISTA C. MAYER THURMAN

The Christa C. Mayer Thurman Curator of Textiles

The Art Institute of Chicago

In 1976 the Art Institute's Department of Textiles acquired a textile and wallpaper sample book, or folio, titled "Schumacher's Taliesin Line of Decorative Fabrics and Wallpapers Designed by Frank Lloyd Wright" (see fig. 1), along with thirteen fabrics of varying lengths. Today, nearly twenty years later, this purchase has proven to be a wise one, for copies of the folio are rare, with only twelve examples known to exist (books of this kind were generally disposed of by the trade and interior designers who would have owned and used them).[1] The folio is an important archival document, with relevance for the department's mid-twentieth-century holdings.

Research into the circumstances surrounding the folio led to fascinating discoveries that one would not normally associate with a commercial product of this nature. The folio raises many issues about the architect's involvement with textile design and the nature of these particular designs, intended for mass production, which were issued toward the end of his long and extraordinary career. While the folio is undated, it was easy to determine that it was published in mid-1955.[2] Of course, the most obvious and immediate question was how Wright, whose contempt for commercialism was legendary, became involved in such an undertaking. The project coincided with the desire of a number of Wright's supporters, among them Elizabeth Gordon, editor of the leading interior-decorating magazine *House Beautiful,* to revive the octogenarian architect's reputation. Toward this end, she determined to dedicate an entire issue of the magazine to an overview of his work in the fall of 1955.[3]

Gordon was also responsible for the idea of introducing a commercial series of Wright-designed textiles at that time. She had managed to secure a number of unusual abstract, hand-painted fabrics, intended as costume material for a theatrical production undertaken by Wright's students (referred to as the Fellowship). Based on the work of the Armenian philosopher Georgy Gurdjieff (1872?–1949), founder of a semireligious movement to which Wright's third wife, Olgivanna, was deeply committed, "Music, Ritual Exercises and Temple Dances" involved a cast of thirty students (the majority of whom were men). The premiere performance took place at Taliesin West, Wright's winter headquarters, in Scottsdale, Arizona. The Fellowship repeated the performance on November 3,

FIGURE 1. Cover, "Schumacher's Taliesin Line of Decorative Fabrics and Wallpapers Designed by Frank Lloyd Wright," 1955 (hereafter referred to in captions as "Taliesin Line" folio). Textile and wallpaper sample book; 58 x 44.5 x 3.5 cm. The Art Institute of Chicago, Restricted gift of Mrs. Theodore D. Tieken (1976.61A [folio], 61B-H, J-O [textiles], 61I [wall papers], and 61P [standing sign]). All works by Wright illustrated in this essay are reproduced with the permission of the Frank Lloyd Wright Foundation. This now rare sample book, intended for trade and interior designers, signals a moment late in Wright's long and extraordinary career, when he agreed to cooperate with several firms to produce commercial products based on his designs. The folio raises many issues about the motives behind the architect's decision, the nature of his involvement with textile designs, and the circumstances of this particular collaboration with F. Schumacher and Company.

1953, at The Art Institute of Chicago's Goodman Theater. Featuring dances, chants, and processions based on Far Eastern mysticism, the production was intended to "explain . . . the creative rituals used in developing talent at Taliesin."[4] The fabrics inspired Gordon to contemplate the manufacture of these striking patterns as marketable yardage. In addition to stimulating interest in Wright, such a project would hopefully yield revenues from royalties to help Wright endow the foundation he had established in 1940.

Gordon contacted her friend René Carrillo, Director of Merchandising at the textile firm F. Schumacher and Company. While he greatly admired the fabrics, he knew immediately that these sophisticated, abstract designs would not have wide commercial appeal. Nevertheless, Carrillo became intrigued by the idea of a line based on designs by Wright, especially if his company could secure a license to use the architect's name in connection with the products. Although Wright endorsed the latest technology and had produced some designs for machine manufacture, it seemed unlikely that he would cooperate, for he always insisted on treating each of his commissions individually, responding to the requirements of patron and the nature of the site. This approach precluded his becoming involved with mass-produced interior appointments throughout the major portion of his career.[5] Nonetheless, overtures were made. First Elizabeth Gordon went alone to see Wright. Thereafter, John deKoven Hill, once an associate at Taliesin and at the time architectural editor at *House Beautiful,* arranged for Carrillo and his wife to go to Taliesin West, where the couple, along with other guests, were graciously and pleasantly entertained one evening. The next day, at a tense but open session, Wright stated that he had never heard of F. Schumacher and Company.[6] He declared unequivocally that he hated decorators and everything about them. He referred to them as "inferior desecrators" and added that he had no interest in anything except architecture. When Carrillo reminded Wright that he had designed furniture for

FIGURE 2. Frank Lloyd Wright (1867–1959). Rendering of living room of B. Harley Bradley House (1900; Kankakee, Illinois). From *Ausgeführte Bauten und Entwürfe von Frank Lloyd Wright* (Berlin, 1911), pl. 22. Wright's desire to fashion a total living space led him to design window treatments, wall surfaces, light fixtures, furniture, tableware, hangings, and carpets, such as the two seen here framing the view of a turn-of-the-century, Mission Style residence for B. Harley Bradley.

FIGURE 3. Frank Lloyd Wright. Rendering of the living room of the Avery Coonley House (1908; Riverside, Illinois). From *Ausgeführte Bauten und Entwürfe* (see fig. 2), pl. 57. In this rendering, a Wright-designed carpet can be seen in the setting for which it was intended.

some of his houses, the architect admitted that he "was a terrible furniture designer and that he had never designed a comfortable chair and that he had become black and blue from sitting in his own furniture."[7]

Nevertheless Carrillo managed to persuade Wright to become involved in the undertaking and to lend his name to the project. "All right," Wright concluded, "we'll do it, but it will be expensive." He obviously knew exactly what he wanted, and he got it: $10,000 up front, twenty-five cents per yard or roll on every yard or roll offered for sale, and $1,000 after approval of each design at the time of its manufacture.[8] These were extremely steep prices in 1954. In addition to financial motives, Wright may have felt the need to make his ideas more accessible to and affordable for the general public, a desire that had prompted him to develop the Usonian House during the later years of the Depression. Based on a modular concept, this design was intended for people with modest incomes.

Founded in New York City in 1889, F. Schumacher and Company was one of the first firms to provide American architects and interior designers with domestically produced decorative textiles. Catering to a broad clientele, not the least of which being the vast carriage trade, it had made its reputation over the years with its conservative, high-quality patterns commissioned from both American and European designers. From 1917 on,

however, Schumacher had also encouraged contributions of patterns from fashionable designers such as Edouard Bénédictus, Donald Deskey, Adolph Griven, Ilonka Karasz, Raymond Loewy, Paul Poiret, Ruth Reeves, and Joseph Urban. In the 1920s, a number of these individuals contributed "modern" designs to the company's products, certainly inspired by the Paris Exposition of 1925, which established the Art Deco style on a grand, international scale.[9]

In the 1950s, Schumacher's product line remained essentially conservative in nature. It included an expanded version of its Williamsburg Collection (designed specifically for Colonial Williamsburg and initially introduced in the 1940s), as well as the Farmer's Museum, the Henry Ford Museum, the Mystic Seaport Museum, and Sleepy Hollow Restoration Collections. Involved with the furnishing-fabric needs of the White House since 1902, the firm also filled special orders in the 1950s for such offi-

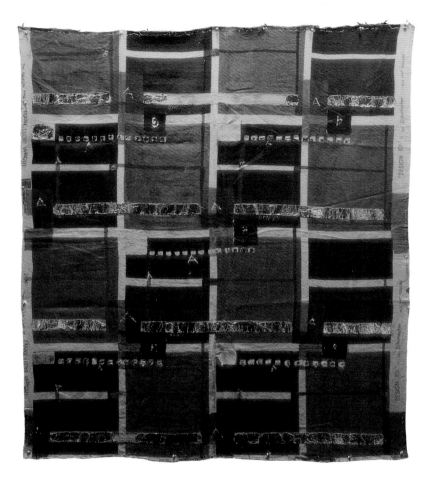

FIGURE 4. Preliminary printed linen sample of Schumacher's design 101, with painted corrections made under the direction of Wright. Photo courtesy of the archives of F. Schumacher and Company.

cial New York State buildings as the State Capitol, the Surrogate Court, and the United States Court House.[10] René Carrillo, who had joined F. Schumacher and Company in 1933, after it bought out his own firm, Carrillo Fabrics, played a major part in persuading the company to pursue more contemporary directions. After the end of World War II, Carrillo became Schumacher's buyer and stylist for printed textiles. While he realized fully the difficulties he would face in collaborating with Wright, he believed that, if properly presented and promoted, a fabric and wallpaper line inspired by Wright's architecture could indeed become successful, for there was little on the market that could be utilized by architects or interior designers faced with the furnishing of contemporary interiors. To Carrillo's delight, Wright and Schumacher reached an agreement. In a letter dated March 22, 1954, Carrillo wrote to the architect: "I was delighted to receive your signed contract, and I approve heartily of using the name 'Taliesin Line.'"[11] But the schedule was tight—if promotional material was to be ready when the special Wright issue of *House Beautiful* reached the newsstands in the fall of 1955, merchandise had to be approved, finished, and stocked by August of that year.

Wright's declaration that he was interested only in architecture was not entirely true. As the noted architectural historian Vincent Scully has written, "Wright was determined to create a new and wholly integrated environment. That style was to encompass everything: so Wright had to 'design' everything. . . . He was like a painter—touching every square inch of his building, inside and out."[12] Wright's involvement with window treatments, wall surfaces, light fixtures, furniture, tableware, and other sorts of decorative objects extended also to fabrics: in particular, designs for carpets and rugs, as well as for curtains, table runners, and other linens that a well-run household required. He also designed scarves and dresses for his first wife and occasionally for some of his female clients, so that even their appearance was consistent with the environment he had created for them.[13]

Other textile designs by Wright can be seen in drawings for a number of his houses. Among the earliest examples are the two carpet designs that flank the rendering of the living room for the B. Harley Bradley House (fig. 2); a design for a large hanging or carpet seen to the right of a drawing for the vaulted, two-story living room of the

Susan Lawrence Dana House (1902–04; Springfield, Illinois); and the large carpet shown in situ in a drawing of the living room of the Avery Coonley House (fig. 3). Later designs include those depicted in the plans for the Imperial Hotel (1912–23; Tokyo), and those for carpets for the F. C. Bogk House (1916; Milwaukee).[14] The Bogk carpets, produced in Czechoslovakia, now belong to the Milwaukee Art Museum, while the original sketches for them, dated by Wright 1914 and 1915, respectively, are in the Frank Lloyd Wright Archives at Taliesin West. When the Bogk House came on the market in 1954, Wright tried to acquire the carpets for a collection relating to his early works that he was interested in establishing at Taliesin. "Beautiful things," he called them in a lecture to the Fellowship. "I said I'd put in new ones, if they'd let me have the old ones and anything they nomi-nated for the place. But no, the rugs had to go with the house." Infuriated that he could not obtain them, he declared, "It seems that the designer of the thing has no caché whatever—no standing in either practice or theory or court. You're only the cuss that did the pattern, that's all."[15] This is a most curious statement from a man who insisted on the integration of all elements of an architectural space; his desire to remove the carpets from the environment for which they had been made is, to say the least, inconsistent with what he stood for! Other textile projects include the Hillside Theatre Curtain, which Wright designed in 1933 for Taliesin East, his summer residence in Spring Green, Wisconsin. Destroyed by fire in 1952, it was replaced by an entirely new design in 1955. The curtain is composed of two Belgian-linen panels, each measuring seventeen by eighteen feet, covered with

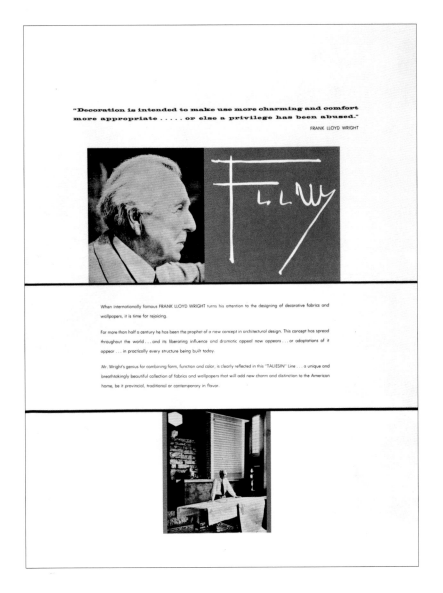

FIGURE 5. "Taliesin Line" folio. The photograph of Wright at his drafting table was taken by Pedro Guerrero.

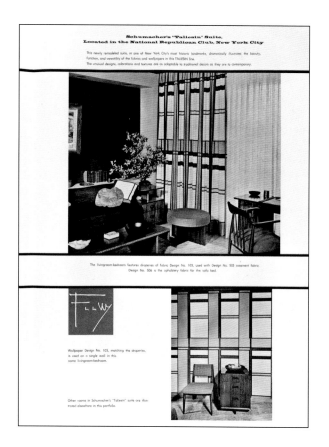

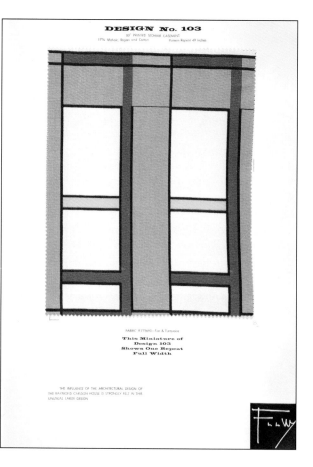

felt, cording, yarns, and lamé. It depicts a highly abstract view of the surrounding landscape.[16]

Wright's intense dislike of interior decorators precluded his working with them. Yet, he needed someone to carry out his wishes and negotiate the details of the production of the furniture and other accessory designs intended for the various complexes he was creating. During the early years of his practice, he turned to Marion Mahony, whom he employed from 1895 to 1911, the year she married the architect Walter Burley Griffin, to take care of such issues. Thereafter, the Milwaukee interior-architecture firm of Niedecken-Walbridge would play a similar role. Throughout his life, Wright's forays into textile design were related to specific commissions, from the custom-designed items for specific residences discussed above to the massive undertaking of designing and supplying machine-produced fabrics for the furniture and interiors designed for the Imperial Hotel.[17]

Thus the Schumacher collaboration constituted something entirely different. First of all, it involved creating repeat patterns based on selected elements taken from existing architectural designs and translating these into silk-screened or woven products. Secondly, it was unre-

FIGURE 6. "Taliesin Line" folio. The four firms involved in the 1955 merchandising effort to create and promote Wright-designed or inspired products were Schumacher, Heritage-Henredon (furniture), Karastan (carpets), and Martin Senour (paints). With the exception of the carpets, which were not manufactured at the time, the products were displayed in several showrooms installed at the National Republican Club, New York. Wright expressed extreme displeasure with the rooms when he saw them, just before the product lines were introduced.

FIGURE 7. "Taliesin Line" folio. The rectangular patterns of Schumacher's design 103 (see also fig. 8) can be found in Wright's R. Carlson House (1950; Phoenix, Arizona), as this page of the folio indicates.

lated to any of his concurrent projects. Wright never intended the "Taliesin Line" for the interiors he designed; if a Schumacher item were to be used in a Wright building, this would be solely the choice of its owner. In the case of his client Ray Ward, Wright used both fabric and wallpaper from the line in the house he built for Ward in New Canaan, Connecticut, in 1956. [18]

Carrillo itemized the company's needs in the above-mentioned letter of March 22:

Our needs for a line to come out in the fall of 1955 would be approximately as follows: *Under Woven Fabrics:* 1. Medium scale design on cotton for upholstery; 2. Light weight textured sheer for glass curtains and for printing; 3. Plain textured material in fairly large color range for woven stripe or plaid or some other type of print that could serve as a filler for the above. *Under Prints:* 1. Fairly large design to be printed on a sheer for large important window spaces; 2. All-over medium size suitable for a slip cover; 3. Small pattern suitable for upholstery or bed spreads and slip covers; 4. Large pattern up to 27" or 28" for curtains; 5. Stripe or plaid that could be printed on the plain textured cloth to go with all the above. *Under Wallpapers:* 1. Large pattern for living rooms.

2. Medium pattern for dining rooms. 3. Medium pattern for bed rooms. 4. Any textured effect appropriate for any type rooms.

The line should consist ideally of four or five wallpapers and some ten or twelve other patterns either print or woven, whichever is your preference.

Carrillo concluded:

As a method of procedure, it might be wise to have you send us rough sketches of anything you may have in mind. We could then have these rough designs put into the finished state, as we would have to have them for either our looms or our various

FIGURE 8. "Taliesin Line" folio. Design 103 came in a number of color combinations.

FIGURE 9. "Taliesin Line" folio. Design 104 (see figs. 10–12) was inspired by the bold, circular rhythms that characterize the homes Wright designed for his sons David (1950; Phoenix, Arizona), and Robert Llewellyn (1951–52; Bethesda, Maryland).

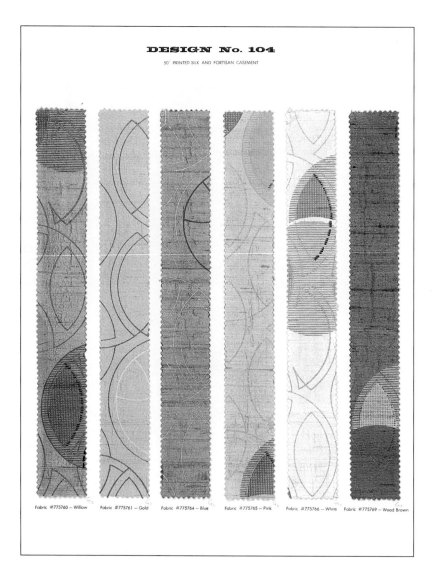

FIGURE 10. Panel (design 104) from the "Taliesin Line." Designed by Ling Po (American, born 1917) for Wright and produced by F. Schumacher and Company, New York, 1955. Rayon and silk, plain weave; screen printed; 296.5 x 126.7 cm. The Art Institute of Chicago, Gift of Brook Davis (1983.176). The pattern's complex interplay of spherical forms, enlivened by playful accents of color, relates to a number of architectural designs Wright produced in his later years (see fig. 9), including the Solomon R. Guggenheim Museum, New York, which was then being constructed.

FIGURE 11. "Taliesin Line" folio. Design 104, offered in six different color combinations, was continued by Schumacher until 1961.

printing processes. These designs could then be returned to you for your final approval and your color suggestions. After getting your final approval, we would have strike offs made and at that time I believe we should make the final selection of our colors.[19]

Wright expressed his feelings about this project in one of his lectures to the Fellowship: "By the way, we've just been commissioned by the greatest company, manufacturing carpets and fabrics, to design a new line—we're going to call it the Taliesin Line of fabrics. So we're now in the fabric industry for the royalty for the designs, and I insisted on a retainer before we would accept. So we now have accepted designs for industry. You can all sit down and make designs to your heart's content. Maybe we'll use them."[20]

Carrillo's narration of the process continues: "We went through all his architectural grammar, old renderings, and ornamentation, we discussed color."[21] By August 1954, Wright saw the first three printed designs and a number of woven patterns. He quickly approved the former but did not find the latter acceptable. As Carrillo recalled, "We were trying for saleability and practicality, while Mr. Wright was trying to be true to his architectural sense."[22] Finally, the problems were resolved after Schumacher submitted their own versions of Wright designs, which the architect evidently found more acceptable and ultimately approved. Included among these was "Desert Cloth," which became one of the line's most successful offerings. (See fig. 4 for an example of a Schumacher design that Wright critiqued and then returned to the company for revisions.)

The folio, part of an edition of one hundred, was sold to authorized dealers only, for $35. Printed and assembled by E. W. Bredemeier and Company, Chicago, it comprises forty-five leaves, with one hundred thirty-seven samples (both printed and woven) and twenty-six wallpaper samples (all printed). The book also contains thirteen larger textile panels—six printed and seven woven—and four wallpapers. Each design is preceded by one or more illustrations (drawings and/or photographs) of the design or design element within Wright's oeuvre that inspired it, as well as a brief text that describes the work's essential features (see fig. 9). This is followed by the design as conceived for and presented in fabric, including a larger sample and smaller cuttings showing additional color choices (see figs. 7–8 and 11), with illustrations of the specific model room in which the fabric and wallpaper were incorporated (see figs. 6 and 12), so that the decorator and prospective client could visualize the line's use. At the back of the book, order forms were included; the sample book was accompanied by a laminated dealer sign attached to a standing support.

The patterns themselves—simple, abstract, and straightforward—can be divided into two categories. The first, which has already been alluded to, are the patterns inspired by Wright that were actually the work of Schumacher's designers (in addition to "Desert Cloth" were designs 501, 502, and 503, among others). The second group, inspired by elements of architectural plans, was designed by Fellows in Wright's studio. Among these are designs 101, 102, and 103 (see figs. 7–8), the work of Ling Po. A Taliesin Fellow since 1946, Po has stated that he made the designs "under the direction and supervision of Frank Lloyd Wright." Furthermore, Po and other Fellows "colored" the designs, again under Wright's direction.[23] The yardage was clearly marked on the selvage with Wright's personal emblem, a terracotta-colored square carrying his initials, "FLLW." This emblem appears throughout the Art Institute's folio (see figs. 1, 5–7, 9, and 12).[24]

Among the most beautiful of the patterns is design 104 (see figs. 10–12), which, as the folio acknowledges, was derived from the plans for two spherical houses Wright designed for his sons Robert Llewellyn and David, in Maryland and Arizona, respectively (see fig. 9). In the pattern's complex interplay of spheres—which has been described as having been created with a compass[25]—can be seen Wright's love of elaborating upon circular shapes (a form he had played with early in the century so successfully in the stained-glass windows for the Coonley Playhouse [cat. no. 9]; and was simultaneously being explored in his dramatic design for the Solomon R. Guggenheim Museum, New York, which was then being constructed). It also reflects his interest in working with forms that he could use in a number of mathematical configurations (such as the design he did for the Heritage-Henredon Company [see below] using geometric elements that could be combined and recombined in various configurations and shapes). While this design, like all of the others in the collection, is basically flat, the surface is charged by the complexity of the overall composition, with its overlapping arcs and partial circles; and a sense of dimensionality is provided by the subtle color choices. A panel acquired by the Art Institute in 1983 (fig. 10) features a palette of delicate gold outlines against an iridescent, light-brown background with strong accents of white and two shades of orange. This striking pattern, offered in six different color combinations, was continued by Schumacher until 1961.

Initially Wright wished to include designs for carpets in this venture with Schumacher.[26] In the address to the Fellowship cited above, he seems to have misunderstood the range of the company's activities, for manufacturing carpets was not part of their program at this time.

The issue was ultimately resolved when the Karastan Rug Mills agreed to produce carpets from Wright's designs. Two design concepts reached the template phase—that is to say, pattern mock-ups were made—but they were a long way from becoming finished carpets. It was not until 1978, when the Grey Art Gallery and Study Center of New York University organized a traveling exhibition entitled "Taliesin Collection," that Karastan actually executed the carpets, so that they could be included in the exhibition.[27] Another product line was developed in connection with the "Taliesin Line": the Martin Senour Paint Company introduced a collection of paint colors that were coordinated with the Schumacher fabrics and wallpapers.[28]

A fourth firm to become involved with Wright's designs was the furniture company Heritage-Henredon. Wright signed a contract for this project on February 15, 1955, almost a year after he had formalized his arrangement with Schumacher.[29] Wright was most unhappy about his cooperative venture with Heritage-Henredon, which produced only one of the three lines of furniture he had designed for the firm. A letter from Wright to the furniture company's Ralph Edwards indicates the architect's displeasure:

From our beginning there has been an indefinable something the matter with Heritage-Henredon where my contract with them goes—and the three lines I laid out for them. I suspect the trouble might be summed up in the word "timidity." I suppose the organization would say "conservative." But so few of my own designs have appeared—no chairs, no tables—none of the good things I expected to see, that I am not surprised at the failure of "the line." The ideas I had to contribute like the unit system of various pieces fitting together into larger and finally quite complete systems of house furnishings never got beyond hassock-small cabinet stage. The more important (to me) tables and chairs were your own idea of what I should have designed.[30]

These various products (except for the carpets) were introduced to the public in the fall of 1955 at a promotional presentation installed in rooms on the fifth floor of New York's National Republican Club (see figs. 6 and 12), conveniently located next to the Schumacher offices on 40th Street. A prominent decorator, Virginia Conner Dick, was selected to design the installation. She was described by Carrillo as "well known, and most likely to typify the type of decorator to whom we [Schumacher] wanted to target the line."[31]

Although the opening and press party apparently took place on October 17, 1955, the Wrights were escorted by Carrillo to the model rooms sometime before September 3. Upon seeing the display rooms with textiles, wallpapers, furniture, and paints bearing his name, Wright

exploded: "My God! An inferior desecrator! I won't permit my name to be used by a decorator. I will have no part of this. You must take off my name. I will tell the world I have been misused."[32] Wright reiterated his position in an undated note (presumably on September 3 or thereabouts) to Carrillo:

My dear René: This is a disagreeable task because I feel it necessary to officially disapprove the exhibition rooms intended to exhibit the designs I made for you . . . in the Republican Club. . . . The spirit of my work has been reduced to the usual tripe, decoration a la mode—only worse because good material is wasted. Nothing of the harmonious unique character of what I did for Schumacher is to be seen there properly used. So kindly refrain from connecting my name with the exhibit—because I wish to be of greater service to you all than this will permit. . . . I would have shown you this if you had referred to me. This you failed to do. . . Affection, just the same. Let's try again.[33]

Carrillo responded:

When we do model rooms, we attempt to show our customers how they can rehabilitate their homes through use of our products. How even with a small investment they can gradually change their style of living. We retain an expert, such as you, so that even the most miserable person, though they can't afford a Frank Lloyd Wright house, can afford a bit of your genius through the use of our products styled by you. Our [rooms are] obviously of mediocre architecture, [as is much of] the average person's home . . . and . . . do not in any sense try to show a Frank Lloyd Wright interior, they are not advertised . . . or promoted as such. . . . Believe me, if you are willing, we would be happy to make a presentation of a Frank Lloyd Wright interior next year, and I deeply hope this will be possible.[34]

Of course it was too late to resolve these problems or to undo the model rooms before their introduction to the trade through this presentation or to the public at large through the pages devoted to the group of designs in the *House Beautiful* issue dedicated to Wright, which apparently was already on the newsstands.[35] The folio was out, and Schumacher had an enormous amount of money tied up in the venture. In the end, Carrillo was "temporarily forgiven" by Wright, but did not hear from the architect for several weeks. When contact was reestablished, the issue was skirted.[36] As references in the correspondence about receipts of royalty checks clearly attest, the line did well.[37] Wright continued to supply new designs to the firm after 1955: specifically, in the spring of 1956, the spring and fall of 1957, the spring and fall of 1958 (another design was actually added to the line in 1960, one year after the architect's death).

Design No. 104 shows Frank Lloyd Wright's adeptness with spherical motifs. In this bedroom, the design is used for the wall-to-wall draperies, and quilted in the same color to make an elegant bedspread.

The Bedroom of Schumacher's "TALIESIN" Suite

FIGURE 12. "Taliesin Line" folio. Among the showrooms installed in the National Republican Club (see fig. 6) was this bedroom, in which design 104 (see fig. 10–11) was utilized so that a decorator and a prospective client could visualize its potential.

References made today to Schumacher's Frank Lloyd Wright textiles encompass many more fabrics and wallpapers than appeared in the initial 1955 folio, as well as carpets (which, as we have seen, did not figure as part of Schumacher's original line), complicating the issue of dating the designs. In addition, other manufacturers copied some of the patterns. Carrillo informed Wright of one such development in a letter sent late in 1956: "I thought you might enjoy seeing a photograph of a copy of our design #103. This has been copied by Fuller Fabrics, and you should be very flattered. I doubt that there is much we can do about this, as they have made just enough changes to keep the copy from being exact, but it is pleasing to know that even our competition admits that you are a pretty fine fabric designer."[38] The Schumacher Company has continued to offer its Wright-associated designs, dropping various patterns over the years. In 1986, the company reissued, in a new collection, a number of

Wright designs, including six printed designs, six sheers or panels, four carpets, thirteen woven fabrics, and six wallpapers. Only two of the textile designs—102 and 705—were part of the 1955 folio.[39]

If Wright's feelings were so strong about the products issued in connection with his name and designs in the 1950s, it is impossible to imagine how he would react to all the various adaptations that have been based on his designs since his death. While copyright laws and licensing agreements regulate such ventures to some extent and help benefit the not-for-profit Frank Lloyd Wright Foundation, it is the vast amount of unlicensed material, loosely inspired by Wright's work, that causes concern and dismay. Yet, this widespread enthusiasm for Wrightian design indicates how pervasive the architect's ideas have become and the degree to which his work remains vital today.

THE LIFE AND WORK
OF MARION MAHONY GRIFFIN

JANICE PREGLIASCO
Architect, Terra Design Group
Mill Valley, California

Marion Mahony Griffin was a founding member of the Prairie School and, aside from Frank Lloyd Wright, the longest practitioner of the movement. Though her architectural renderings defined and publicized the Prairie style throughout the world, and though the buildings that she designed stood on three continents, she is virtually unknown today. In the United States, her built projects are often attributed to Wright, who claimed some of them during his lifetime. In Australia and India, her designs are credited to her husband Walter Burley Griffin, another Prairie School architect. Fortunately, The Art Institute of Chicago has the largest collection of Marion's drawings and projects in the world, as well as her autobiographical manuscript "The Magic of America," and these materials reveal her sculptural and architectural designs, her artistic mastery, and her passionate beliefs.

As a six-month-old baby, Marion Lucy Mahony was carried from the Great Chicago Fire of October 1871 in a clothes basket to Hubbard Woods north of the city. There she fell in love with the natural world and developed a taste for adventures. Her idyllic childhood ended at age eleven with her father's suicide. Marion's mother became a Chicago school principal to support her five children, a highly professional position for a woman in the nineteenth century. The Mahony home on Chicago's West Side became an artistic haven. Every day of the week was given over to neighborhood art classes, dramatic rehearsals, orchestral groups, and poetry studies.

Marion as an adolescent was tall, with a beaked nose, bright, closely set eyes, and a distinctive low voice. Intelligent and expressive, she emphasized her ideas with dramatic arm gestures. After completing high school, Marion followed her cousin, Dwight H. Perkins, to the Massachusetts Institute of Technology School of Architecture. The class of 1894 boasted only eight women out of 270 freshmen; Marion was the only non-Bostonian. Her dislike for the academic European models she was required to study caused her to fail the sophomore design studio by a single point. She excelled in the rigorous, Beaux-Arts-modeled drawing classes, even supplementing them with extracurricular art classes in Boston. She became only the second woman to earn a bachelor's of architecture degree at MIT.

Unlike most female architectural students of that era, Marion succeeded in landing an apprenticeship after graduation. Perkins hired her while he was in a rush to complete construction drawings for the Steinway Piano Company headquarters in Chicago's Loop. The building's attic loft became Perkins's office, which he shared at one time or another with most of the members of the Prairie School, including Wright.

Marion joined Wright's young practice in 1895 as "superintendent" of a non-existent drafting force.[1] Shortly thereafter, Wright began plans for an architectural office attached to his home in suburban Oak Park, a project

FIGURE 1. Marion Mahony Griffin (1871–1962), c. 1890s. Photo courtesy of the Frank Lloyd Wright Home and Studio Foundation (H214). Marion Mahony Griffin was one of the founders of the Prairie School. As an architect, she designed some of the finest Prairie-style buildings. As a delineator, she produced remarkably beautiful drawings that helped establish the reputation of the Prairie School.

FIGURE 2. Marion Mahony Griffin, designer. *Window from the Gerald Mahony House, Elkhart, Indiana,* 1907. Clear, opaque, and iridescent leaded glass; 61 x 76 cm. The Art Institute of Chicago, Restricted gift of David C. Hilliard and the Department of Architecture Purchase Fund (1984.193). This was one of the windows that Marion Mahony Griffin designed for an addition to her brother's farmhouse, which became her weekend retreat for many years.

recalling Marion's MIT thesis, "A House + Studio for an Artist." Marion designed the unique capitals for the entrance-loggia columns; each featured a sculptural relief of a tree (of knowledge), a book of specifications, and an unrolled drawing of the studio's floor plan. Bracketing them are two tall, solemn storks, called "wise birds (architects)." The open book and the storks were Marion's contributions; she gave Wright photographs of the storks on the condition that they be used as the entrance motif.

The first decade of the twentieth century saw the flowering of the Prairie style in Wright's studio. His most famous landmarks, including the Robie, Dana, Martin, Heurtley, and Coonley houses, and the Larkin Building and Unity Church, were built in those years. By this time, Marion was the studio's most senior member and its most vivid personality. She had a corner table in the octagonal drafting room, and coworkers recalled that her "mordant humor . . . promised an amusing day."[2] Wright's son John, a child at the time, was intimidated by Marion: "[She] was so ugly and her laugh so boisterous that I was afraid of her. Later, after seeing and appreciating her beautiful drawings, I thought her beautiful."[3] Marion became Wright's sounding board for his architectural ideas, especially in refining his ideas for his 1901 keynote lecture, "The Art and Craft of the Machine." According to the sculptor Richard Bock, Marion was "a brilliant intellectual and a match for Wright in debate. She served as a source of practice and training for his lecturing."[4]

The studio apprentices developed the detailed portions of a project—the interior, art-glass windows, stairs, fireplaces, mosaics, murals, furnishings, and lighting —into integrated parts of the project's concept. In-house competitions were held for these designs, sometimes extending to the floor plans and elevations themselves. "Miss Mahony" won most of them.[5] Many of these winning designs were kept in notebooks for reference for future projects, explaining the evolution and consistency of the office's style during this defining period of the Prairie School. Wright jealously guarded credit for the designs; sharp reprimands followed any reference to "Miss Mahony's design."[6]

Marion recounted her design of two residential plans while at the Wright studio:

Early in my architectural career I was told to work out some economical plans for homes. Among the attempts was one which satisfied me as a solution. It was shown to my architect employer [Wright] and filed for use when the occasion came. . . . The scheme was the basis of a number of subsequent houses varying largely in such particulars as number of rooms, type of roof and motif of details.[7]

Marion referred to her plans as "experiments" to break away from the ubiquitous rectangular box. She gave the rectangle first arms, then wings:

My next amusement was a still further break from the parallelogram. My reception room was on ground level and projected from the center of the front. Broad steps led from it to the level of the main living rooms which assumed a T shape, the stem being the kitchen quarters back of the living rooms. One day later Walt [Griffin] called on me to spend the evening, and in the course of it said that he and Wright had a competition for the plan and that Wright had won. I laughed and told him that it was I who had won, for it was my plan that Wright had used in that competition. The Walser house was built to that plan.[8]

Marion's plan placed the public rooms across the front. Upstairs, the stem held the bedrooms, giving the public rooms below a double-height volume. This layout gave a small house the spaciousness and feeling of a much grander residence. The plan became the basis of many of Wright's Prairie residences; traces can be found in designs through his Usonian houses of the 1950s. Marion used the plan in 1912 for her own home as well. By extending the center room forward and shifting it slightly off-center, she transformed the T into a pinwheel. Marion used the pinwheel plan for all her post-Wright residences.

The Wright studio made perhaps its greatest contribution to the melding of art and architecture in the realm of art glass. In Prairie homes, continuous bands of windows made of beautiful and richly colored patterns of art glass formed the upper half of walls.[9] Scores of glass designs emerged from the Wright studio during the fifteen years of its existence, and Marion was the prime producer of these designs.[10] Wright would determine the decorative motif for the project, and Marion would then develop the theme and variations into the project's elements. Conventionalized plant forms, chevrons, and small squares, common design themes in her independently designed windows (see fig. 2), are present in virtually every major Wright building of the period, including the Dana, Robie, Martin, Bradley, Coonley, and Heath homes, and Unity Temple. Marion's glass designs frequently fea-

FIGURE 3. Marion Mahony Griffin, delineator. *Thomas P. Hardy House, Racine, Wisconsin,* 1905; perspective from Lake Michigan. From *Ausgeführte Bauten und Entwürfe von Frank Lloyd Wright* (Berlin, 1911), pl. 15. This rendering, which Marion produced while she worked in Frank Lloyd Wright's studio, is the most famous Prairie School architectural drawing. The affinities between Japanese aesthetics and Prairie School design are apparent in this drawing, particularly in the asymmetrical placement of the house and in the emphasis on the flower below.

FIGURE 4. Marion Mahony Griffin, delineator. *E. H. Cheney House, Oak Park, Illinois,* 1904; aerial perspective. From *Ausgeführte Bauten und Entwürfe von Frank Lloyd Wright* (Berlin, 1911), pl. 30.

tured patterns that carried across a group of windows to be resolved at the bracketing ends. This technique created a group of windows as an architectural unit. Such designs are found in the Martin, Heath, Bradley, and Coonley houses, as well as Marion's Amberg House. This concept is not found in any other Prairie architect's work.

Marion designed the windows of the Frederick C. Robie House (1907; Chicago), one of Wright's most important works.[11] She used one of her favorite motifs, the home's roof line, as the basis for the geometric, abstract designs of diamonds and triangles. From this basic motif, Marion developed variations for each aspect of every room; there are five different patterns in the hall alone. The upper part of the windows, the portion seen above the terrace walls, received the lion's share of the design and colored glass to increase privacy from nearby pedestrians. The intense shades of gold, violet, turquoise, rose, red-brown, and green iridescent glass used here were typical of Marion's bold and unusual color palette.

Marion's designs for furniture for the E. P. Irving House encompassed everything from Prairie-styled grand pianos to grandfather clocks.[12] But the most original piece is a combination couch/table/desk/lamp. In plan the piece resembles a miniaturized version of Marion's pinwheel houses. The cantilever-topped oak desk anchors the public side of the room. The cross axis holds an art-glass light and functions as the head board for the couch, which is cantilevered beyond the plane of the desk. The piece allowed two people, one working at the desk and one reading on the couch, to both enjoy the fireplace. Integrating furniture functions was an extension of the built-in furniture; they kept the open room uncluttered, and demarcated functional areas within them. Marion was the only architect besides Wright to use furniture as an architectural element.

Marion's distinctive presentation drawings are her most recognized contribution to the Prairie School. Her overlapping double-M monogram, or Wright's handwritten notes regarding her authorship, appear on several of the Wright studio's presentation drawings. Her renderings became important tools in publicizing Wright's career, appearing as magazine illustrations, in exhibitions and in an influential monograph of Wright's early work. Interestingly, the art historian Eileen Michels noted a "marked improvement" in the quality of Wright's published drawings beginning with the Francis Apartments rendering, Marion's first project with Wright.[13]

The architect Barry Byrne, a key member of the Wright studio, attested to Marion's remarkable technique. According to an essay written by Byrne, "The style of these drawings of Miss Mahony's was determined only in a general way by Mr. Wright, he having in mind, of course, the artistic character evident in Japanese prints.

The picture compositions were initiated by Miss Mahony, who had unusually fine compositional and linear ability, with a drawing 'touch' that met with Mr. Wright's highly critical approval." He continued:

Exception might here be taken of the word "executed" as possibly implying close direction by Wright. There was stimulation, approval, and supplementing accord, but not what one could call close direction. Mr. Wright would occasionally sit at Marion's board and work on her drawings, and I recall one hilarious occasion when his work ruined the drawing. On that occasion Andrew Willatzen, an outspoken member of the staff, loudly proclaimed that Marion Mahony was Wright's superior as a draftsman. As a matter of fact, she was. Wright took the statement of her superiority equally.[14]

There are clear differences between Wright's and Mahony's drawing styles. Wright drew with rulers and triangles, Mahony drew freehand. Wright's foliage followed geometric shapes, but Mahony's was naturalistic. Wright favored color pencil on paper; Mahony, ink and color washes on fabric. While the MIT/Ecole des Beaux Arts compositional style of overlapping planes of perspective, plan, and section continued in Marion's later work, it is missing from Wright's office drawings after her departure.

Marion's brilliant presentation styling of Wright's Prairie houses began in 1902. The pen-and-ink drawings shared common elements that would become Marion's signature style throughout her career. The presentation was narrowly rectangular and asymmetrical. The drawing pushed up or to the side of the paper, a compositional device of Japanese prints. Below the perspective were small floor plans shown staggered, stacked, or side by side.

Marion's sympathetic integration of architectural and natural forms transmitted the core values of the Prairie movement. By connecting foliage masses in her drawings, she transformed nature into a series of dramatic scrims for a building. Nature functioned in her renderings as the frame, foreground, and background. Marion often used trees as a vertical counterpoint to the horizontality of the Prairie homes and as the springboard for the framing line. In her drawings, the framing line often dissolves with the landscape pouring through the gaps. Plants establish the foreground plane, setting up a tension that pulls the eye to the building. Dense woods or strands of trees fill the background in even suburban settings. Nature never stopped at the doorstep—Marion brought it to the building with overflowing urns, long planter boxes under windows, and flowering vines climbing over gates and spilling over balconies.

Because Marion emphasized the intense delineation of the landscape, building materials are rarely rendered.

Her buildings function as the negative, restful interlude in abundant, dynamic nature. The most intensely rendered areas of the building are the windows. Windows are the permeable membranes between inside and outside in a building, and Marion often emphasized this fact by showing one or more windows thrown open. A breeze often catches a drape, blowing its hem outside the window.

One of the finest qualities of Marion's art is the contrast between the free, intricate movement of linework describing the natural world, and the crisp, angular, linework used for the buildings. The landscape is delicately and freely drawn; walls and roofs are indicated in broad, sharp lines.

Marion always chose the most dramatic viewpoint for a project. Many homes on flat midwestern sites were given a slight upward perspective, a child's-eye view, to enhance the monumentality of the house. Houses situated on hills were almost always shown rising above the observer to the top of the paper.

The perspective view of the Thomas P. Hardy House (fig. 3) is the defining rendering of the Wright studio and one of the most evocative and compelling architectural drawings ever produced. It is little more than three inches wide and is composed mainly of empty space. The house is seen from the lake below. A delicate, flowering branch is introduced midway up the page. Less than a half dozen lines describe the lake, shore, and cliff. At the uppermost edge of the paper is a house of planes and tall windows perched dramatically atop the bluff. The sky above is described by parallel lines.

The eye is first captured by the beauty of the flower, then moves upward to the majesty of the house. All is done with supreme simplicity and delicacy of line. The asymmetrical placement of the house on the page, the emphasis on the primacy of the flower, and the striated rendering of the sky are all attributes of Japanese prints. No drawing better represents the profound sympathy between Japanese art and Prairie School architecture.

A second notable example is the E. H. Cheney House rendering (fig. 4). To give the low-slung house an assertive presence amid taller neighbors, the first floor was raised and a long wall designed across the front. The terrace wall gave the house a sense of privacy, but a street level view would show nothing. As seen in the drawing, Marion rose in her imagination above the sidewalk to show us the intimate home that lay beyond the wall. One of the many French doors to the terrace is open, giving a glimpse of the living room. The foreground trees hover with us; trailing vines ascend the trunk of one, while delicate flowering shrubs are seen below. The viewpoint is a child's treetop view of the home, the perspective Marion often took of her own home in Hubbard Woods.

FIGURE 5. Marion Mahony Griffin, architect. All Souls Church, Evanston, Illinois, 1903. Interior, pulpit and chancel. In this church, which was the first of Marion's built projects, she designed everything, and even executed the painting of Christ on the chancel's wall.

Marion's renderings became the basis of roughly half of the plates in *Ausgeführte Bauten und Entwürfe von Frank Lloyd Wright*, a portfolio of Wright's work printed by the German firm Wasmuth (see cat. no. 32). According to the architectural historian Vincent Scully, it is "one of the three most influential architectural treatises of the twentieth century."[15] H. Allen Brooks, one of the foremost scholars of the Prairie School, wrote of the Wasmuth portfolio:

Of the delineators, Marion Mahony was unquestionably the most prolific. Judged in terms of the Wasmuth drawings, she contributed nearly half of those which appear attributable. There are some seventy-two plates with architectural perspectives and, of these, at least twenty seem to be primarily by her hand.[16]

Byrne, who kept an annotated copy of the monograph, attributed over half of the plates to her drawings.

The Wasmuth portfolio demonstrates that Marion was the dominant member, aside from Wright himself, of the most influential American architectural practice of the early twentieth century. Wright's biographer of his early career, Grant Carpenter Manson, called Marion "the key figure" of the staff at Oak Park: "If the Studio had been organized along more conventional lines, she would have held the rank of head designer." Robert C. Twombly, another Wright biographer, said Wright "delegated enormous responsibility" to Marion Mahony. Barry Byrne considered Marion, "the most talented member of Frank Lloyd Wright's staff, and I doubt that the studio, then or later, produced anyone superior."[17]

A few months before Wright's departure to Europe in 1909, he asked Marion to carry on his commissions in Chicago, but she refused, as did several other colleagues. Shortly thereafter, Wright gave the job to Hermann von Holst, a recent arrival at the Steinway Hall loft who had been two years behind Marion at MIT. Wright's contract with von Holst requested that he "retain as far as is practicable the services of Mr. Wright's assistants." Von Holst, an architect unversed in the Prairie style, naturally turned to Marion. "After [Wright] had gone," Marion wrote, "Mr. von Holst, who had taken over, asked me to join him, so I did on a definite arrangement that I should have complete control of design. That suited him." Marion established a division of six draftsmen in von Holst's office to handle the commissions. Because Wright was incommunicado, Marion was free to create for herself: "For this period I had great fun designing."[18]

Marion's first solo project, All Souls Church in Evanston, Illinois (fig. 5), was built in 1903. Marion's first design linked three geometric forms—a cube, a rectan-

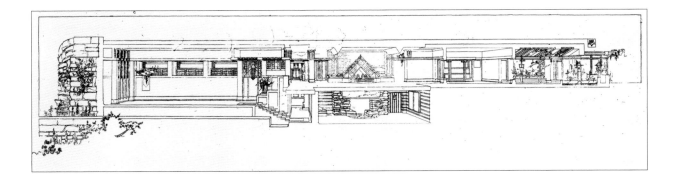

FIGURE 6. Marion Mahony Griffin, architect. *Henry Ford Estate, Dearborn, Michigan,* 1913; section/perspective. Ink on linen; 55 x 189 cm. Mary and Leigh Block Gallery, Northwestern University (1985.1.118).

gle, and an octagon, and resembled the design of Wright's studio. The building committee rejected it, calling for something "more Gothic." Marion was able to retain more of her original design on the interior.

The focus of a church is the altar, and in Marion's design it was a stunning stage. The pulpit was raised and framed by a tall arch with a shallow chancel behind. Both the pulpit and the chancel featured art-glass skylights across their curved ceilings. Above the pulpit, Marion designed a white bird flying from a circle on a rectangular shaft. It cast an unearthly light on the pastor below that no stage spotlight could surpass. The bands of colored light from chancel's skylight appeared to radiate from the head of the resurrected Christ that Marion painted on the chancel's rear wall.

Two important new commissions came to the von Holst office after Wright's departure: a house in Detroit for the designer of the Model T, Childe Harold Wills; and another house for Wills's boss, the inimitable Henry Ford (see cat. no. 8). The size and scope of these commissions would, if built, rival the largest and most lavish of Wright's Prairie homes of the previous decade. Marion had an unprecedented opportunity to give the Prairie School two new residential landmarks.

The Wills house was the first project Marion designed for von Holst. The home's exterior vertical elements are typical of Marion's work, with tall, narrow piers separated by narrow slots of delicate art glass, elements and proportions that are totally unlike Wright's. The floor plan is an innovative combination of formal and informal, and of outside and inside. The projecting living room terminates on a large fountain whose waters cascade both inside and out. The view down the long

entry concludes with an open conservatory that bridges the formal enclosed dining room and the informal breakfast porch.

The best aspects of Marion's design for Henry Ford's estate are seen in her dramatic section perspective of the interior (fig. 6). The music room was located a half level between the main and lower floors. The semicircular end of the room featured a series of tall fins with decorative recesses. The open stairs to the room were given a lacy lattice ceiling and wall of elaborately patterned art glass recalling the square-and-triangle motif of the exterior tiles. The living room was an original: triangular beams run across the ceiling and a triangular fireplace with triangular iridescent tile occupies the main wall. Downstairs, the cliff face dramatically protrudes into Ford's private den as a rough masonry wall and rustic fireplace.

Three homes in downstate Decatur, Illinois, for the brothers Robert and Adolph Mueller and E. P. Irving form the largest grouping of Mahony residences in the world. Adolph Mueller's house (fig. 7) is most purely hers. Crisp, spreading gable roofs straddle the two-story axis of the dining and master bedroom and the flanking low pavilionlike entrance porch. The long upper roof stops short of the lower, giving the composition a sense of impending flight. Anchoring the house to the earth is a high concrete base. Windows run in bands separated by small piers. Their art-glass design takes its form from the clean angle of the gable.

In the interior of the Adolph Mueller House, a wide entrance hall bisects the living and dining rooms, an arrangement with no Wrightian counterpart. Folding art-glass doors demark a small den at the end of the hall. When not in use, the den's three large art-glass windows

terminate the entry's view. The living room's tented ceiling reflects the roofline above and is lit by two winglike art-glass ceiling lights. Art-glass doors lead to the living porch. A dark wood band at door height runs throughout the first floor, tying together living, entrance, and dining rooms, zigging out to form open shelves. Wood grilles covering air vents mirror the art-glass window designs.

Upstairs the house is no less intriguing. Narrow art-glass windows of clear, white, and gray glass light the stair landing. The upstairs hall is lined with built-in cupboards. Stained-glass windows face into a special mink room for Mrs. Mueller. The end wall of the tent-ceilinged master bedroom is made of delicate pieces of clear, pink, and white art glass mirrored in the glassed-in sleeping porch just beyond. Prodigious amounts of light pour through this double set of windows.

Marion's 1909 home for the David Ambergs in Grand Rapids, Michigan, included furniture and linens, making it the most complete house built to her design (fig. 8). The house was published in the October 1913 issue of *The Western Architect*, and was so widely admired that both von Holst and Wright would later claim it as their own. Marion used the lot's existing embankment to construct a two-story building that appears to have only one story. An arm of the house, a brick wall, comes out to the sidewalk. At the end is a low-roofed entry. Inside the low dark vestibule is a stairway that, upon ascending, turns to face a wall of delicate yellow and clear glass windows. For someone living in this house, this sequence—of

FIGURE 7. Marion Mahony Griffin, architect. Adolph Mueller House, Decatur, Illinois, 1910; view of exterior. Photo: Mati Maldre, Chicago. The design of this house is particularly notable for its dramatic gable roofs and its bands of art-glass windows.

first being exposed to light, then sheltered from it, and finally ascending into it—made the everyday act of coming home a transcendental experience.

A pattern of piers and voids is found throughout the Amberg House. At the top of the stairs, a wood beam spans the opening between two piers to the tented living room. By sinking the living room a few steps, Marion added height to the large room. A tall wall of art-glass windows gives the space the countenance of a church. To the left, glass doors lead to a roofed porch. To the right, stairs between two massive piers lead up to the dining room. Both rooms have intricate patterned colored-glass skylights recessed in the ridge of the ceiling.

An important clue to discerning a design by Marion is her use of color—she was the freest of all the Prairie architects in this regard. She used, for example, green roof tiles with deep red-brown brick; contrasting bands of orange, beige, and dark brown or red brick; and color ceramic tiles to relieve or accentuate wall areas. As an artist and designer she mastered color and its combinations, and was bold in their use. Color often signals her design presence in Wright projects, as in the striated brick banding in the Heurtley House and the ceramic tile walls of the Coonley House from Wright's office.

The Amberg House is a perfect example of Marion's attention to color. Red-brown brick, yellow plaster, brown roof tiles, and verdigris copper surround multicolored tiles inset under the eaves that mirror the colored glass of the windows.

Marion designed the Ambergs' table lamps, rocking chairs, couch, tables, umbrella stands, picture frames, beds, and rugs. The dining-room chairs featured broad slat backs with narrow voids at the sides, a design that was equivalent to the pier-and-void combination found in the exterior and interior architectural elements of the house.

All five of Marion's projects for von Holst share common design elements unique to her among the Prairie architects. The floor plans are variations of a long main axis of public rooms terminating in outdoor terraces. A secondary axis of private rooms was set off-center at a right angle, resembling a pinwheel and reflecting the characteristic gesturing of her long arms. The plans reach out, with terraces or outdoor rooms at their ends to embrace nature. The "casual" arrangement of the rooms gives the plans an informal character perfectly suited to family life.

The interiors of Marion's Amberg and Mueller houses are more architectonic and sculptural than Wright's E.P. Irving House (1909; Decatur, Illinois) and Meyer May House (1908; Grand Rapids, Michigan). The division between living and dining spaces is articulated by piers, columns, changes in floor levels, and ceilings. In the Irving and May homes, the same floor and ceiling are used, and there is minimal division of space between the two rooms. Also characteristic of Marion's designs are her sharp, low gable or hipped roofs with flat, extending eaves, often expressed on the interior as tent-like ceilings. As in Wright's designs, windows are grouped in horizontal bands pushed up just under the eaves, a design element she admired in the Ho-o-den building at the 1893 World's Columbian Exposition, with its "immense quantities of light and air."[19]

When she joined von Holst's office, Marion was reunited with the Steinway Hall gang, including her cousin Dwight Perkins and a friend from the Wright studio, Walter Burley Griffin. Walter's independent practice had emphasized landscape architecture, his true love. Marion hired Walter to design the landscape of the common areas between the Mueller and Irving residences. Marion's regard for Walter's ideas developed into infatuation. Marion was, as she wrote, "swept off my feet in delight in his achievements in my profession, then through a common bond of interests and intellectual pursuits, and then with the man himself. It was by no means a case of love at first sight, but it was a madness when it struck."[20]

Their courtship was staged on the Chicago River and surrounding waterways. They purchased a white canoe, christened "Allana," for a systematic adventure: the

FIGURE 8. Marion Mahony Griffin, architect. David M. Amberg House, Grand Rapids, Michigan, 1909; front view. Photo: *Western Architect* 20, 10 (Oct. 1913). This house was so widely admired that Wright and the architect Hermann von Holst both took credit for its design.

RESIDENCE FOR MR. D. M. AMBERG, GRAND RAPIDS, MICHIGAN
H. V. VON HOLST, ARCHITECT, CHICAGO. MARION M. GRIFFIN, ASSOCIATE

J.C.MELSON
DWELLING
MASON CITY IOWA
SCALE:----

Walter Burley Griffin Architect

investigation of all the streams and rivers of the greater Chicago area. They slept in canvas bags, Marion getting Allana as her mattress.

Though Marion and Walter's relationship was a meeting of minds, physically and temperamentally they were opposites. Marion was tall, angular, dark, energetic, and "a brilliant, fiery, passionate person"[21] with a scathing wit. Walter was short, round, blond, passive, imperturbable—a gentle philosopher. Both were romantic idealists who saw the Prairie School as a means to portray the ideals of American democracy in three-dimensional form. Both were inclined toward political reform, and were early supporters of Henry George's single tax on land values. And both loved untrammeled nature. They eloped in June of 1911, marrying in one of their favorite places, the Indiana Dunes on the shore of Lake Michigan.

During their courtship, Marion offered her design services to Walter, and within months she assumed the management of his office. Historians have noted the sudden maturity of Walter's architecture beginning in 1910.[22] Walter's movement away from Wrightian-inspired idioms to a more personal style was directly related to his professional and romantic collaboration with Marion.

Barry Byrne, who worked with both Walter and Marion at Wright's studio and later became their partner, felt their marriage was an artistic union as well as a personal one. Roy Lippincott, who worked for both before and after their marriage, agreed: "She had great influence upon his work. . . . Their two minds seemed to provide inspiration to each other. . . . There was the closest accord between them."[23] As in the Wright studio, Marion was the design talent of Walter's office. Byrne noted, "While I had high regard for Marion's talent, I did not have like regard for Walter's. . . . The imaginative element was largely hers."[24] Lippincott agreed: "When it came to detail and pattern she was supreme and he [Walter] seldom or never suggested any alterations."[25]

Their largest project was seventeen houses designed for a development in Mason City, Iowa, called Rock Crest/

Rock Glen. It remains today as the largest group of Prairie School buildings unified by a common site. It became the crowning achievement of Marion's architectural delineation, as well as the Griffins' work in the United States. Marion's bird's-eye perspective rendering is a masterpiece (cat. no. 10). She divided a six-and-a half-foot-long satin panel into a triptych of two narrow sides flanking a long, horizontal main panel. Both houses and the architectonic pedestrian bridge were painted white against the muted autumnal tones of the landscape. The ink lines are subtle and easily dominated by the planes of color that blend almost indecipherably into the pale green satin. The effect is that of a warm, hazy autumn afternoon.

The landscape is at once oriental and idealized, yet faithful to actual conditions. Nature is elevated over architecture. The delineation of the site's trees are as individual and distinctive as the houses. No trees are "cut" from the drawing, even if they obscure most of the home's street facade. The focus of the composition is a river, not a building. No drawing better summarizes the Prairie School's emphasis on the landscape as the inspiration for architecture.

The masterwork of the development was produced for Marion's friend J. G. Melson, a previous Wright client. Like the famous Hardy House perspective, Marion's rendering of the Melson residence (fig. 9) views the house from the water below, effectively moumentalizing a modest cube of a house. Once again a delicate natural form—here a flowering branch—leads us into the drawing. The branch obscures the reflection of the house in the river, leading our eye upward to the house itself. Instead of an austere cliff, we see a rich shoreline of rushes and a cliff overgrown with trees and bushes. Site plan and floor plan float inconspicuously on the river; the contour lines of the site plan becoming ripples in the water. Marion's twisting vines grow out of the cliff and onto trellised overhangs above the balcony and windows. Unlike Wright, who clarified his landscape with architecture, Walter wanted to nestle his houses into an untouched nature. Marion portrayed the Melson house as an outgrowth of its site.

The first house Marion designed for herself (fig. 10) was at the focal point of a thirty-home development Walter was planning called Trier Center in Winnetka, Illinois, near Hubbard Woods. Two pairs of chimney-like piers with a slit of space in between define the entrance to the house. The remainder of the exterior is made entirely of windows. Narrow triangles and chevron-shaped perforated concrete tracery with inset opalescent glass form the entire second floor of the house. One can imagine the beauty of the colored light shapes on the floor of the living room below. Triangular mullions create a zigzag pattern on the eave of the concrete slab roof.

FIGURE 9. Marion Mahony Griffin, delineator. *J. G. Melson House, Mason City, Iowa,* 1912; perspective and plans. Ink on linen; 94 x 55 cm. Mary and Leigh Block Gallery, Northwestern University (1985.1.120). This house is the masterpiece among the seventeen houses that Marion and her husband Walter Burley Griffin designed for Rock Crest/Rock Glen, a development in Mason City, Iowa. In this rendering, Marion depicted the Melsons, her husband, and herself picnicking on the low terrace.

In April 1911 the competition Walter had waited for all of his professional life was announced: the design of the new capital city of Australia, Canberra. Yet it was Marion's threat not to draw a line of the competition drawings that induced a procrastinating Walter to begin their submission six months later. He envisioned a city in a garden. His ideas on defining axes and symbolic geometry were clearly manifested in his city plan and a series of explanatory diagrams.

Marion gave Walter's concept a communicable picture, a vision. Her submission drawings consisted of perspectives of the Federal Triangle area, the center of the capital, and long elevations. The elevations perfectly conveyed the city's relationship to the land and illustrated how future buildings would accentuate hills with landmarks such as the capitol, the cathedral, the arsenal, and the university. More clearly seen in the unrendered pen-and-ink versions, Marion's drawings were a blueprint of how future buildings should be designed and situated to fulfill the symbolic intent of Walter's plan.[26]

Marion's submission panels were dazzling and compelling. Eight feet wide and up to thirty feet long, the elevations continued across several hinged panels, unfolding like Japanese screens. The presentation easily filled a large room. It was so seductive that the judges had small reproductions made so as to not to be swayed by the originals.

On May 23, 1912, Walter was declared the winner out of 137 entrants. Marion's work was cited by several contemporary accounts as a major factor in the decision. The London *Town Planning Review* felt that Marion's drawings swayed the verdict in their favor:

We have only reproductions of the originals before us, but are struck by the beautiful though somewhat eccentric method of presentment which Mr. Griffin has adopted in his drawings. It is quite possible that the Board of Assessors may have been carried away with the mere charm of this display. We certainly must offer Mr. Griffin our congratulations on his drawings, and his great success.[27]

Walter was appointed Director of Design and Construction of Canberra in October of the following year. The Griffins sailed to Sydney in June 1914 with members of their office staff. Before long they were operating three far-flung offices: Barry Byrne managed the Chicago office, Marion the Sydney office, and Walter the Federal Capital office in Melbourne, 550 miles away. Marion designed all of the private Australian projects.

Marion transplanted the Prairie School to the very different climate and landscape of Australia. The three architectural masterpieces of the Griffins' Australian career were designed by Marion: Cafe Australia, Newman College, and the Capitol Theatre. Cafe Australia, the Griffins' first private commission in 1915, was the first example of modern architecture on the continent.

As in her residences, the entry to the cafe set the stage. Receding white square arches with deep blue and gold tile insets above represented the night sky. A transparent glass entry led into the gold and ivory interior of the restaurant. As in her Midwest residences, Marion divided the space into a series of distinct architectural "islands" with piers and skylights. The most remarkable elements are three sculptural piers (fig. 11) of stylized trees—an almond, a cherry, and an orange—that separate the fountain court from a grand stairway. Emerging from the opposite side of the piers are three women stepping through shafts of tall grain. The piers are a singular merging of architecture and sculpture.

For the restaurant, Marion designed tables with slender inverted wood supports and tops bordered with rich woods. Each chair had an inverted teardrop-shaped open back, a round wood frame leather seat, and slender flaring wood legs. Marion designed the restaurant's china, which featured a stylized pattern of the balcony design connected by a ring of small triangles. She also designed the flatware and menus.

For Newman College, a new Catholic college at the University of Melbourne, Griffin laid out the horizontal, Prairie-style buildings in quadrangles surrounding interior gardens. Marion's hand is most purely sensed in her design for the refectory rotunda, which soars above the long dormitories.[28] The refectory's dome is made of intersecting low and tall arches that define a square opening (lantern) at the center. In the lantern, pairs of arched windows let in a surprising amount of daylight. The lantern is crossed diagonally with buttresses of three slender spires in ascending height, which are known as the twelve apostles. In the center rises a diamond-shaped stone spire, a design foreshadowed in Marion's Canberra drawings.

The chapel at the center of the campus refined all the decorative elements of the rotunda (fig. 12). Four stone

FIGURE 10. Marion Mahony Griffin, designer. *House of Walter Burley Griffin and Marion Mahony Griffin, Winnetka, Illinois,* 1912; perspective, plans, section, and elevation. Ink on linen; 94 x 57 cm. Mary and Leigh Block Gallery, Northwestern University (1985.1.108). This house was part of Trier Center, a thirty-home development that Walter Burley Griffin planned for Winnetka. Trier Center was never built because of the Griffins' departure for Australia to design the city of Canberra.

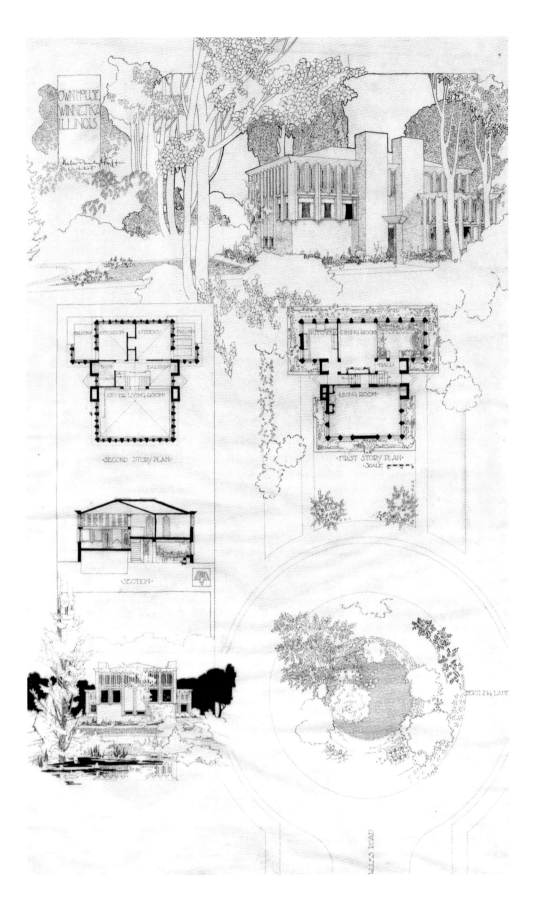

OWN HOUSE
WINNETKA
ILLINOIS

·SECOND· ·STORY· ·PLAN·

·FIRST· ·STORY· ·PLAN·
·SCALE·

·SECTION·

FIGURE 11. Marion Mahony Griffin, architect. *Cafe Australia, Melbourne, Pier Design*, 1915. Hectograph print on paper; 25 x 48 cm. The Art Institute of Chicago, Gift of Marion Mahony Griffin through Eric Nicholls (1990.57.2). In its combination of architecture and sculpture, this design displayed Marion's considerable talents as both a designer and an artist.

piers defined the corners of the rectangular nave. Between them were not walls, but windows of slender, triangular ribs rising to form spires. Instead of leaded glass, Marion used a richly ornamented perforated concrete screen inset with iridescent colored glass, similar to her Trier Center house design. The pattern formed both the walls and the ceiling, integrating the church interior. Inside, benches facing the center aisle were crowned with wooden versions of the spires, completing a space of rare ornamental complexity in a spatially simple shape. It was at once Gothic and profoundly modern. The church was built to another design, which was a great loss to architecture.

In 1921 the client who commissioned Cafe Australia hired the Griffins to design a ten-story building across from the Melbourne City Hall. The Capitol Building encompasses both an office building and a 2,000-seat theater, with the theater protruding from the back of the tower. The vast majority of the drawings made for the building—over 400—are signed by Marion.[29]

The streetside facade is a restrained and well-proportioned design of Prairie and Chicago School idioms. Six plain rectangular piers frame large square windows, each divided into four smaller squares. The upper squares are in turn divided into an even finer pattern of square panes. Squares as the decorative motif are carried to the street level in the canopy, glass lights, and the entry ceiling.

In contrast to this concert of squares is the theater lobby beyond: all swoops and curves, arches and domes. Stairways from the theater above pour sinuously into the entry, disgorging its patrons much as water from a stream. The tunnel-like stairs and their hidden lighting prepares theatergoers for the cavelike wonders within. The theater auditorium is all angles, prisms, and crystals. The vast ceiling is formed of receding, stepping rec-

tangles dissolving into "walls" that are themselves three-dimensional. Covering both walls and ceilings are over 33,000 plaster crystals, each perforated with geometric patterns. The crystals seem to gather and culminate in a huge cloud that pours down the proscenium over the stage. Marion turned a functional necessity—acoustical diffusion—into a work of organic art.

But the pièce de résistance occurs when the house lights dim. The crystals dissolve into a pulsating man-made sky, a symphony of color created by 6,000 red, green, blue, and white light bulbs hidden inside the ceiling crystals (fig. 13). Their prismatic shapes reflect the colored light on neighboring crystals, dissolving and intensifying them. The ceiling becomes a force of nature, conveying the visual experience of a sunset, the Northern Lights, or fireworks in a night sky. It is one of architecture's most dazzling experiences. The apparent dematerialization is accomplished in a space forcibly physical and three-dimensional.

The visual motifs in the Capitol Building are metaphorically related to its functions. The squares of the facade represent the rational world of commerce, the physical world outside. The sensuous curves of the lobby are an architectural directive to abandon the rational world and enter the emotional one of the theater, which forms a vast crystal "cave." In the 1920s, crystals were commonly viewed as symbols of transformation, especially among German architects. Marion made the pedestrian act of leaving a downtown sidewalk and entering a theater one of architectural transcendence.

After the successful opening of the Capitol Theatre in 1924, Marion went into semiretirement in a deliberate attempt to refocus architectural attention on her husband.[30] Marion moved to Castlecrag, the couple's new community development in Sydney. At Castlecrag she completed a series of "tree portraits," and became a saleswoman for the development as well as the community's spiritual, educational, social, and artistic leader. She produced and directed over a dozen dramatic productions in her own outdoor amphitheater.

Few of Walter's designs were built in the ensuing decade. In 1935 he was called to India to design a library for the University of Lucknow. Because of additional new projects, Walter asked Marion to join him in India a few months later. The radically different climate and culture of India inspired numerous design inventions and reenergized her own architectural work. In less than a year Marion would design over one hundred buildings.[31] Screens, domes and pyramids, cubes and ovals, rhythmic and stepped designs filled her drawing board. Marion's organic forms and decoration contrasted sharply with the imperial style of British architects designing in India, and continued the Prairie style long after the Prairie School had waned in the American Midwest.

A prime example is the Canopy Pavilion for the United Provinces Exhibition of Industry and Agriculture. Three interlocking, almost Gothic arches of bamboo formed the sides of the pavilion. A stylized pattern of bamboo leaves filled the arches. Other bamboo strands were woven together to form columns and a curved roof. At the end of the building, a single bamboo arch

FIGURE 12. Marion Mahony Griffin, designer. *Newman College Rotunda, Melbourne, Australia,* 1916; section through dome. Black and brown ink on linen; 93 x 105 cm. The Art Institute of Chicago, Gift of Marion Mahony Griffin through Eric Nicholls.

extended to form a canopy over the entering fairgoers. Of such delicacy that it appeared to be made of reeds and paper, the building was a lovely and appropriate form for the forestry section of the fair, reflecting the deep sympathy Marion felt for trees.

Marion's design for the University of Lucknow Student Union (fig. 14) emphasized the building's function by glorifying movement. Featuring entrances on all sides, tall arches framed open stairs that carried the eye diagonally up to scrolling incised lines of the roof. The form is monumental in repose and dynamic in occupancy—a perfect blend of form and function that highlights both the importance of the students' building and its role as the hub of the campus.

In the midst of this renewed creativity, Walter died suddenly in February of 1937 from the effects of a gall bladder that had ruptured earlier at Castlecrag. Marion completed their Indian projects and returned to Sydney a few months later. After settling Walter's estate, which was found to be in debt, she sailed home to Chicago after virtually a twenty-five-year absence.

Her professional focus in the United States turned to city planning, a natural extension of her strong political, environmental, and educational concerns. Marion's plans for new communities in New Hampshire and Texas show Walter's influence. The plan for the World Fellowship Center in New Hampshire, for example, recalls Canberra with its emphasis on views and its handling of hillsides. The artistic community of Crystal Hills, Texas, owed more to Walter's conception of Castlecrag with its

layered dwellings and unobstructed views of the water below, and its large, connecting community-owned natural areas. Marion's client for these communities, Lola Maverick Lloyd, fell ill shortly after the Crystal Hills plan was completed and died the following year. Marion's plans were therefore never realized. Yet they represent the first communities in the world designed entirely by a woman.

In 1947 the Chicago *Herald* sponsored a competition called "A Better Chicago." Marion's entry, made when she was seventy-six, is her last known architectural design. The site was a large section of the South Side of Chicago. Marion replaced rectangular blocks with a large, circular community building in the center of each neighborhood surrounded by pentagonal blocks with interior parks. Commercial or public buildings anchored the corners of these blocks; houses with staggered setbacks filled in between. Encircling these blocks were large, Y-shaped blocks of sport fields and tennis courts that were to be shared by the neighborhoods. Marion's plan—never executed—was a radical departure from the relentlessly perpendicular divisions of land in the Midwest.

Marion spent the late 1940s writing her memoirs, a book she hoped would publicize Walter's work in America. She never found a publisher. With the deaths of her sister and nephew occurring in quick succession, Marion donated the materials documenting her career to The Art Institute of Chicago, and to other institutions and universities, and raised her niece's three young children. Marion died in 1962 at the age of ninety.

FIGURE 13. Marion Mahony Griffin, designer. Auditorium Ceiling of the Capitol Theatre, Melbourne, Australia, 1924. Photo: Mati Maldre, Chicago. When the lights are dimmed in the Capitol Theatre, the effect of the 6,000 red, green, blue, and white light bulbs inside the ceiling crystals is dazzling.

LUCKNOW UNIVERSITY
UNION BUILDING.
MICROFILM FRAME NO. 293

Marion's spaces reflected her own dramatic and dynamic nature. She masterfully choreographed the elements of each entryway in her buildings. Once inside one of her buildings, a visitor could never enter a room without being lead up or through or down or under. Marion's development of the pinwheel brought this dynamism to the most static element of architecture, the plan, and it is her most telling innovation.

Ornament was an integral, organic part of Marion's designs. In her view, a decorative motif and its repetition throughout a structure was a basic unit of architectural composition. No design motif was added for its own sake. She often used ornament to reinforce the lines of the structure. As she matured, her ornament became increasingly sculptural and three-dimensional, as can be seen in the perforated wall/screens of her design for Trier Center, the sculptural islands of Cafe Australia, the enveloping three-dimensional form of the Capitol Theatre, and the freestanding sculpture of the Lucknow Student Union.

Marion Mahony Griffin was the greatest architectural artist of her generation, which included men such as Wright, Charles Rennie Macintosh, Sir Edwin Lutyens, and Adolf Loos, and perhaps in American history. She was recognized as such by colleagues. Charles E. White, Jr., wrote to an architect friend, "I think she is one of the finest in the country at this class of rendering."[32] Roy

FIGURE 14. Marion Mahony Griffin, designer. *Lucknow University, Student Union Building, Lucknow, India,* 1936; preliminary exterior perspective. Graphite on yellow tracing paper; 76 x 62 cm. The Art Institute of Chicago, Gift of Marion Mahony Griffin through Eric Nicholls (1990.391.1). In this design, monumentality meets movement. With the Student Union Building, Marion succeeded in creating an Indian (and democratic) response to the Paris Opera House.

Lippincott considered her "the finest architectural draftsman this country has produced."[33] The English architectural critic Reyner Banham called her "America's (and perhaps the world's) first woman architect who needed no apology in a world of men."[34] The range and effect of her spaces are extraordinary, from the airiness of the Mueller House master bedroom, the architectural division of the Amberg House living and dining rooms, and the sublime transcendence of the Newman College rotunda to the crystalline wonder of the Capitol Theatre and the dynamism of the Lucknow University Student Union. These are masterful and singular spaces ranking with the greatest achievements of the Prairie School.

NOTES

TWOMBLY, "Foreword," pp. 84–91.

1. Frank Lloyd Wright, "A Home in a Prairie Town," *Ladies Home Journal* 18 (Feb. 1901), p. 17.

2. James S. Ackerman, *The Villa: Form and Ideology of Country Houses* (Princeton, N.J., 1990), p. 9.

3. Frank Lloyd Wright, "In the Cause of Architecture," *Architectural Record* 23 (Mar. 1908), p. 155.

4. James F. O'Gorman, *H. H. Richardson: Architectural Forms for an American Society* (Chicago, 1987), pp. 113–23.

5. Of the thirteen, one for Willimantic, Connecticut (1883) was not constructed. A fourteenth, so far unidentified and undated, is known only from a drawing, but seems to conform to the pattern described in this text. A fifteenth proposal, for altering a station not of his design in Boston, was also unexecuted.

6. The best study of these issues remains Leonard K. Eaton, *Two Chicago Architects and Their Clients: Frank Lloyd Wright and Howard Van Doren Shaw* (Cambridge, Mass., 1969).

WILSON, "Prairie School Works in the Department of Architecture," pp. 92–111.

1. Nancy K. Morris Smith, ed., "Letters, 1903–1906, by Charles E. White, Jr., from the Studio of Frank Lloyd Wright," *Journal of Architectural Education* 25, 4 (Fall 1971), p. 104.

2. See Kevin Nute, *Frank Lloyd Wright and Japan* (London, 1993); and Clay Lancaster, *The Japanese Influence in America* (Rutland, Vt., 1963).

3. Wright's essay was originally presented as a talk in March 1901 at Hull House, reprinted in Bruce Brooks Pfeiffer, ed., *Frank Lloyd Wright: Collected Writings* (New York, 1992), vol. 1, pp. 59, 61, 65. On the Arts and Crafts connection, see Richard Guy Wilson, "Chicago and the International Arts and Crafts Movements: Progressive and Conservative Tendencies," in John Zukowsky, ed., *Chicago Architecture, 1872–1922: Birth of a Metropolis*, exh. cat. (Chicago, 1987), pp. 209–28.

4. See H. Allen Brooks, "'Chicago School': Metamorphosis of a Term," *Journal of the Society of Architectural Historians* 25, 2 (May 1966), pp. 115–18; C. Matlack Price, "Secessionist Architecture in America," *Arts and Decoration* 3 (Dec. 1912), pp. 51–53; Arthur C. David, "The Architecture of Ideas," *Architectural Record* 15 (1904), pp. 363–64; and Hugh Garden, "A Style of the Western Plains," in Henry Saylor, ed., *Architectural Styles for Country Houses* (New York, 1919), pp. 101–11.

5. Frank Lloyd Wright, "Organic Architecture," *Architect's Journal* (London, 1936); reprinted in Frederick Gutheim, ed., *Frank Lloyd Wright on Architecture* (New York, 1941), p. 187.

6. An important ingredient in the acceptance of the term was the publication by Wilbert and Marilyn Hasbrouck of *The Prairie School Review* from 1964 to 1981.

7. See Richard Guy Wilson and Sidney K. Robinson, *The Prairie School in Iowa* (Ames, Iowa, 1977); and Minnesota Museum of Art, *Prairie School Architecture in Minnesota, Iowa, Wisconsin*, exh. cat. (St. Paul, Minn., 1982).

8. According to H. Allen Brooks, *The Prairie School: Frank Lloyd Wright and His Midwest Contemporaries* (Toronto, 1972), the Prairie School came to an end in 1916.

9. Richard Guy Wilson, "Themes of Continuity: The Prairie School in the 1920s and 1930s," in Wilson and Sidney K. Robinson, eds., *Modern Architecture in America: Visions and Revisions* (Ames, Iowa, 1991), pp. 184–213.

10. Victor Marie Charles Ruprich-Robert, *Flore ornementale* (Paris, 1876), p. 2.

11. The important studies of Sullivan's ornament from this period include Wim de Wit, ed., *Louis Sullivan: The Function of Ornament*, exh. cat. (New York, 1986); Paul Sprague, *The Drawings of Louis Henry Sullivan: A Catalogue of the Frank Lloyd Wright Collection at the Avery Architectural Library* (Princeton, N.J., 1979); and Theodore Turak, "French and English Sources of Sullivan's Ornament and Doctrine," *Prairie School Review* 11, 4 (1974), pp. 5–29.

12. John Vinci, *The Trading Room: Louis Sullivan and the Chicago Stock Exchange* (Chicago, 1989).

13. The best study is Larry Millett, *The Curve of the Arch: The Story of Louis Sullivan's Owatonna Bank* (St. Paul, Minn., 1985).

14. The fullest background can be found in Lauren S. Weingarden, *Louis H. Sullivan: A System of Architectural Ornament According with a Philosophy of Man's Powers* (New York, 1990).

15. Background on the Ponds can be found in John Zukowsky and Pauline Saliga, *Chicago Architects Design: A Century of Architectural Drawings from The Art Institute of Chicago* (Chicago, 1983), p. 92; and Henry F. Withey and Elsie Rathburn

Withey, *Biographical Dictionary of American Architects (Deceased)* (Los Angeles, 1970), pp. 478–79.

16. H. Allen Brooks, "Steinway Hall, Architects and Dreams," *Journal of the Society of Architectural Historians* 22, 3 (1963), pp. 171–75.

17. Irving K. Pond, "The Life of Architecture," *Architectural Record* 18 (Aug. 1905), pp. 144–60; and idem, *The Meaning of Architecture: An Essay in Constructive Criticism* (Boston, 1918), p. 175.

18. "The Work of Tallmadge and Watson, Architects," *Western Architect* 22, 6 (Dec. 1915), p. 47; reprinted in H. Allen Brooks, ed., *Prairie School Architecture: Studies from "The Western Architect"* (Toronto, 1975), p. 268. See also Brooks (note 8), pp. 102–04.

19. Thomas E. Tallmadge, "The Chicago School," *Architectural Review* 15 (Apr. 1908), pp. 69–74.

20. Reprinted as Hermann Valentin von Holst, *Country and Suburban Homes of the Prairie School Period* (New York, 1982); see pls. 10, 15–17.

21. See Cheryl Robertson, *The Domestic Scene (1897–1927): George M. Niedecken, Interior Architect*, exh. cat. (Milwaukee, 1981).

22. See Brooks (note 8), pp. 149–50, 161–64; and Kathryn Bishop Eckert, *Buildings of Michigan* (New York, 1993), p. 119.

23. Frank Lloyd Wright, *An Autobiography* (New York, 1977), p. 185. See Theodore Turak, "Mr. Wright and Mrs. Coonley," in Wilson and Robinson, eds. (note 9), pp. 144–63.

24. Of the many studies of Wright's life, the best is Robert C. Twombly, *Frank Lloyd Wright: An Interpretative Biography* (New York, 1973).

25. Marion Mahony Griffin, "The Magic of America" (unpub. ms.), Ryerson and Burnham Libraries, The Art Institute of Chicago, section 13, p. 1 et seq. The basic sources on this project are Robert E. McCoy, "Rock Crest/Rock Glen: Prairie School Planning in Iowa," *The Prairie School Review* 5, 3 (1968), pp. 5–39; and Wilson and Robinson (note 7), pp. 10–16.

26. See Donald Leslie Johnson, *The Architecture of Walter Burley Griffin* (South Melbourne, 1977); and Sidney K. Robinson and Elizabeth A. Scheurer, *The Continuous Present of Organic Architecture* (Cincinnati, 1991), pp. 21–22, 69.

27. Berry's former wife, Mrs. Grace Berry Mueller, quoted in Donald L. Hoffman, "The Brief Career of a Sullivan Apprentice: Parker N. Berry," *Prairie School Review* 4, 1 (1967), pp. 7–15; this article contains virtually the only information on Berry.

28. The Midway Gardens, 1914–1929, exh. cat. (Chicago, 1961).

29. Anthony Alofsin, *Frank Lloyd Wright—The Lost Years, 1910–1922: A Study of Influence* (Chicago, 1993), pp. 59, 140–50.

30. Frank Lloyd Wright, *An Autobiography* (New York, 1977), pp. 205–06.

31. Joseph Griggs, "Alfonso Iannelli: The Prairie Spirit in Sculpture," *Prairie School Review* 2, 4 (1965), pp. 5–23.

32. See Sharon Darling, *Chicago Ceramics and Glass: An Illustrated History from 1871–1933* (Chicago, 1979), pp. 125–26; and idem, *Chicago Furniture: Art, Craft, and Industry, 1833–1983* (New York, 1984), p. 252.

33. The principal study of Maher's career is J. William Rudd, "George W. Maher: Architect of the Prairie School," *Prairie School Review* 1, 1 (1964), pp. 5–11. Cathy Cummings of Chicago is preparing a full-length study of Maher.

34. The best sources on Byrne are Sally Anderson Chappell, "Barry Byrne: His Formative Years," *Prairie School Review* 3, 4 (1966), pp. 5–23; and idem, *Barry Byrne, John Lloyd Wright, Architecture and Design* (Chicago, 1982), pp. 8–38. See also Brooks (note 8), pp. 81–82, 319–29.

BARTER, "The Prairie School and Decorative Arts at The Art Institute of Chicago," pp. 112–33.

1. Mark Hammons, "Purcell and Elmslie, Architects," in Michael Conforti, ed., *Minnesota 1900: Art and Life on the Upper Mississippi, 1890–1915* (Newark, Del., 1994), p. 219.

2. George T. B. Davis, "The Future of House Decoration," *House Beautiful* 5 (May 1899), p. 266.

3. Kevin Nute, "Frank Lloyd Wright and the Woodblock Print: The Geometric Abstraction of Natural, Man-Made and Social Forms," *Andon: Journal of the Society for Japanese Arts and Crafts* 45 (1993), pp. 3–14.

4. Edward S. Cooke, Jr., "George Washington Maher," in Wendy S. Kaplan, ed., *"The Art That Is Life": The Arts and Crafts Movement in America, 1875–1920*, exh. cat. (Boston, 1987), p. 391; and Leslie Greene Bowman, *American Arts and Crafts: Virtue in Design*, exh. cat. (Los Angeles, 1990), p. 92.

5. Frank Lloyd Wright, *Writings and Buildings*, ed. Edgar Kaufmann and Ben Raeburn (New York, 1960), p. 300.

6. Frank Lloyd Wright, "In the Cause of Architecture: Second Paper," *Architectural Record* 35, 4 (1914); reprinted in Frederick Gutheim, ed., *In the Cause of Architecture: Essays by Frank Lloyd Wright for Architectural Record, 1908–1952* (New York, 1975), p. 122.

7. Frank Lloyd Wright, "In the Cause of Architecture," *Architectural Record* 23 (Mar. 1908), pp. 155–221.

8. H. Allen Brooks, *The Prairie School: Frank Lloyd Wright and His Midwest Contemporaries* (Toronto, 1972), pp. 10–11.

9. David Kendall was the principal designer and manager of the Phoenix Furniture Company from 1879 until his death in 1910. During his early career as a draftsman for the Bromley, Hunn, and Smith Furniture Company, he studied drawing, painting, mechanical drawing, architecture, sculpture, and modeling. Before going to Grand Rapids, Kendall worked for William Wooton, maker of the patented Wooton desk. He worked in Chicago from 1873 to 1879 and was perhaps in the employ of the Fairbanks Furniture Company. Kendall joined the Phoenix firm in 1879 and was soon made a designer. He founded his own furniture company in Detroit in 1886, but returned to Phoenix in 1889 as chief designer. For further information on Kendall and the Phoenix Furniture Company, see Kaplan, ed. (note 4), pp. 150–51; Frank E. Ransom, *The City Built on Wood: A History of the Furniture Industry in Grand Rapids, Michigan, 1850–1950* (Ann Arbor, Mich., 1955); and Jane Perkins Claney and Robert Edwards, "Progressive Design in Grand Rapids," *Tiller* 2, 1 (Sept.-Oct. 1983), pp. 35–37.

10. Claney and Edwards (note 9), p. 48.

11. It appeared in a Frank Lloyd Wright house in Wilmette, Illinois, and the Trellis Room at the Colony Club in New York, decorated by Elsie de Wolfe. See Robert L. Ames, "A West Suburban House," *American Homes and Gardens* (Mar. 1912), p. 88; Elsie de Wolfe, *A House in Good Taste* (New York, 1913), p. 270; and "Before and After," *House Beautiful* 17, 5 (Apr. 1905), p. 32.

12. The stenciled number underneath the seat rail of the Art Institute's chair corresponds to numbered furniture designs now in the library at the Kendall School of Design in Grand Rapids; the number authenticates this chair as one manufactured by the Phoenix firm. The chair design was one of only three to be patented by Phoenix. The patent was filed on July 24, 1897 (pat. no. 27,597); see Claney and Edwards (note 9), n. 37. Joseph McHugh and Company of New York, Paine Furniture of Boston, and J. S. Ford, Johnson of Chicago all copied the chair design for their trade catalogues. See Kaplan, ed. (note 4), p. 150, cat. no. 35; and Don Marek, *Arts and Crafts Furniture Design, 1895–1915*, exh. cat. (Grand Rapids, Mich., 1987), pp. 29–30.

13. Claney and Edwards (note 9), pp. 43–45. For more information on the Belgian finish, or others Kendall developed, see "Modern Finishes," *Michigan Artisan* (1904), p. 4.

14. Sharon Darling, *Chicago Furniture: Art, Craft, and Industry, 1833–1983* (New York, 1984), p. 114. Research on the Art Institute's Ford, Johnson chair was provided by Seth A. Thayer III, Luce Fellow in the Art Institute's Department of American Arts.

15. A. T. Andreas, *History of Chicago* (Chicago, 1886), vol. 3, p. 735; and Darling (note 14), p. 115.

16. In 1904, the year the Art Institute's chair was introduced, the firm reportedly sold over 21,000 square feet of chairs. To aid in the production and distribution of their products, the firm acquired several other businesses, including: Philander Derby and Company of New York and Boston, and the Hitchcock Chair Company of Indiana, both of which produced Ford, Johnson designs, and the Stoller and Barnes Company of Chicago, which specialized in the sale and distribution of chairs. See David A. Hanks, *High Styles: Twentieth Century American Design* (New York, 1985), p. 57; and Andreas (note 15), p. 735. A similar chair in the collection of the Wolfsonian Foundation, Miami, bears the paper label of the Philander Derby Company of New York.

17. J. S. Ford, Johnson and Company, *Fiber Rush, Imported Malacca and Mission Furniture: Special Catalogue, 1904–1905* (Chicago, 1904). This volume is in the collection of the Winterthur Museum Library, Winterthur, Del.; a photocopy is in the files of the Department of American Arts, The Art Institute of Chicago.

18. Hanks (note 16), p. 57.

19. Letter from Dr. Barry Harwood, Associate Curator of Decorative Arts at The Brooklyn Museum, to the Department of American Arts, The Art Institute of Chicago, May 1, 1995.

20. Other Ford, Johnson chairs of this design are in the Baltimore Museum of Art, The Brooklyn Museum, The Metropolitan Museum of Art, the Victoria and Albert Museum, and the Wolfsonian Foundation collection.

21. In discussing his approach to architecture, Maher wrote: "The fundamental principle [is] to receive the dominant inspiration from the patron, taking into strict account his needs, his temperament and environment, influenced by local color and atmosphere in surrounding flora and nature. With these vital impressions at hand, the design naturally crystallizes and motifs appear which being constantly utilized will make each object, whether it be of construction, furniture or decoration, related" (George W. Maher, "A Plea for an Indigenous Art," *Architectural Record* 21, 6 [June 1907], p. 433). This quotation also appears in Robert Judson Clark, ed., *The Arts and Crafts Movement in America* (Princeton, N.J., 1972), p. 66.

22. Edward S. Cooke, Jr., "George Washington Maher," in Kaplan, ed. (note 4), p. 396.

23. Darling (note 14), p. 250.

24. William Gray Purcell described watching Elmslie design these screens. See William Gray Purcell Papers, Correspondence [C:124], Northwest Architectural Archives, University of Minnesota

Libraries, St. Paul. Quoted in Hammons (note 1), pp. 220–21, n. 19.

25. David Gebhard, "William Gray Purcell and George Grant Elmslie and the Early Progressive Movement in American Architecture from 1900 to 1920" (Ph.D. diss., University of Minnesota, 1957).

26. Elmslie's furniture was fabricated by Jean B. Hasswer Company, Chicago; John S. Bradstreet and Company, Minneapolis; and George M. Niedecken, Milwaukee, Wisconsin. This chair bears no manufacturer's label, but is marked on the rear rail with the number 3.

27. Hammons (note 1), p. 256; letter from David Gebhard to Milo Naeve, Aug. 12, 1976, Curatorial Files, Department of American Arts, The Art Institute of Chicago.

28. Kaplan, ed. (note 4), p. 204.

29. Darling (note 14), p. 256.

30. The clock is described in William Gray Purcell, *Parabiography for 1912*, commission 142b, located in the Architectural Records, Purcell and Elmslie Archives, William Gray Purcell Papers, Northwest Architectural Archives, University of Minnesota Libraries, St. Paul. A blueprint drawing of the clock with the architects' embossed seal was in the George M. Neidecken Collection of the Prairie Archives, Milwaukee Art Museum, and is now in a private collection.

31. Alan K. Lathrop, "The Prairie School Bank: Patron and Architect," in *Prairie School Architecture in Minnesota, Iowa, Wisconsin* (St. Paul, Minn., 1982).

32. See Kaplan, ed. (note 4), p. 204; and Kirk Varnedoe, *Vienna 1900: Art, Architecture, and Design,* exh. cat. (New York, 1986), pp. 78–79, 82–83.

33. See *House Beautiful* 9 (Dec. 1900), pp. 2–8; and *House Beautiful* 10 (Oct. 1901), p. 322.

34. Entry by W. Scott Braznell in Kaplan, ed. (note 4), p. 278.

35. Sharon S. Darling and Gail Farr Casterline, *Chicago Metalsmiths: An Illustrated History,* exh. cat. (Chicago, 1977), p. 61.

36. The club was named after the ancient cliff-dwelling Indians of the Southwest whose culture and aesthetics were aclaimed. Consequently, the name was chosen for a club of art-minded, modern Chicagoans who also had studios and workshops in tall office buildings. See Edward Thomas Hill, "The Cliff Dwellers of Chicago" (M.A. thesis, De Paul University, 1953), p. 9.

37. George Grant Elmslie's wife, Bonnie, worked in Jarvie's shop, and Elmslie executed some designs for Jarvie commissions. Those commissions, such as the trophy and commemorative book for the retiring University of Michigan president (1909), are far more organic, naturalistic, and curvilinear. See Edward J. Vaughn, "Sullivan and Elmslie at Michigan," *Prairie School Review* 6, 2 (1969), pp. 22–23.

38. See *First Exhibition of the Chicago Arts and Crafts Society,* exh. cat. (Chicago, 1898), p. 133; and Alan Crawford, *C. R. Ashbee* (New Haven, Conn., and London, 1985), pp. 96–98.

39. Entry by W. Scott Braznell in Kaplan, ed. (note 4), p. 280.

40. Wright gave his address "The Art and Craft of the Machine," on March 1, 1901, to the Chicago Arts and Crafts Society. It was reviewed in the *Chicago Tribune* on March 4, 1901, and reprinted in the exhibition catalogue of the Chicago Architectural Club in 1901. The date of the lecture was erroneously published by Brooks (note 8) as March 6.

41. See esp. Philip Webb's library table, illustrated in David A. Hanks, *The Decorative Designs of Frank Lloyd Wright* (New York, 1979), p. 34.

42. Most of his furniture designs prior to 1907 were manufactured by cabinetmaker John W. Ayers of Chicago. See David A. Hanks, "Introduction: The Art and Craft of the Machine," *Frank Lloyd Wright: Art in Design* (New York, 1983), pp. 10–11.

43. See Coy L. Ludwig, *The Arts and Crafts Movement in New York State, 1890s-1920s* (Hamilton, N.Y., 1983), p. 106.

44. Christopher Dresser, *Principles of Decorative Design,* 4th ed. (London and New York, [c. 1880]), p. 57.

45. See Leslie Greene Bowman, *American Arts and Crafts: Virtue in Design,* exh. cat. (Los Angeles, 1990), pp. 92–93.

46. Leonard K. Eaton, *Two Chicago Architects and Their Clients: Frank Lloyd Wright and Howard Van Doren Shaw* (Cambridge, Mass., 1969), pp. 82–84.

47. John Lloyd Wright, *My Father Who Is on Earth* (New York, 1946), pp. 41–42.

48. John Ayers's workshop burned in 1907, and Wright used Neidecken-Walbridge for furniture manufacture after that date.

49. Nancy Morris Smith, ed., "Letters, 1903–06, by Charles E. White, Jr., from the Studio of Frank Lloyd Wright," *Journal of Architectural Education* 25, 4 (Fall 1971), pp. 104–12.

50. See Cheryl Robertson, *The Domestic Scene (1897–1927): George M. Niedecken, Interior Architect,* exh. cat. (Milwaukee, 1981), pp. 69–94. Niedecken was not a cabinetmaker, but he made drawings for

furniture factories. Many of his renderings were manufactured by the F. H. Bresler Company.

51. Jonathan Lipman, *Frank Lloyd Wright and the Johnson Wax Buildings* (New York, 1986), p. 88.

52. Ibid., p. 91.

WOOLEVER, "Prairie School Works in the Ryerson and Burnham Libraries," pp. 134–51.

1. Letter from Burnham Librarian, unsigned, to Daniel Catton Rich, director of the Art Institute, Feb. 7, 1944, The Art Institute of Chicago Archives.

2. In 1981 the Department of Architecture was established with the transfer of 40,000 drawings from the Burnham Library's collection. Remaining in the Ryerson and Burnham Libraries' archives are the photograph collections, business and personal papers, and all published documents.

3. Reminiscing about his childhood interests, Wright recalled an early enterprise called "Wright, Doyon and Lamp, Publishers and Printers," and rhapsodized about the printing process: "Is anything more pleasurable to the mind than unsullied paper? The studious comparisons and selection of 'stock' in textures and colors of cards and paper? . . . The choice of type—a range of choice to tease the most ample taste. The absorbing mechanics of actual press work. What room for space invention—'composing'!" (Wright, *An Autobiography* [New York, 1943], p. 36).

4. In 1893 Wright designed Winslow's River Forest, Illinois, residence, where Wright and Winslow printed *The House Beautiful*. Winslow was also one of five investors to establish the Luxfer Prism Company, maker of patterned glass block, for which Wright prepared over forty patented designs in 1897. See Thomas Heinz, *Frank Lloyd Wright: Glass Art* (London, 1994).

5. The Art Institute holds copy number 45 of the ninety copies of the latter title, which was received in 1926 from the estate of the architect Howard Van Doren Shaw. A more complete discussion of Wright's publishing projects placed in the larger context of book design and production at the turn of the century is contained in Mary Jane Hamilton, *Frank Lloyd Wright and the Book Arts,* exh. cat. (Madison, Wis., 1993).

6. In 1886 Wright's uncle Jenkin Lloyd Jones commissioned Joseph Lyman Silsbee (later Wright's first employer in Chicago) to design Unity Chapel in Helena, Wisconsin. Gannett wrote about the construction of the project in "Christening a Country Church," *Unity* 17 (Aug. 28, 1886). See Robert L. Sweeney, *Frank Lloyd Wright: An Annotated Bibliography* (Los Angeles, 1978), p. 1. *Unity* was published by Gannett's friend Jenkin Lloyd Jones, who was also Wright's uncle.

7. John Lloyd Wright, *My Father Who Is on Earth* (New York, 1946), p. 42.

8. Robert C. Spencer, Jr., "The Work of Frank Lloyd Wright," *Architectural Review,* n.s., 3, 6 (June 1900), p. 70.

9. The design historian David A. Hanks proposed a hypothesis on the symbolism of the title pages: "The roots of the tree are entwined with stylized branches and leaves that form both a landscape and a connecting pattern through which the figures walk. The young Apollonian figure symbolizes the architect while the block he holds on his head symbolizes integrity" (Hanks, *The Decorative Designs of Frank Lloyd Wright* [New York, 1979], p. 176).

10. The "Wasmuth portfolio" must be distinguished from another Wasmuth book on Wright published in 1911. The smaller format *Frank Lloyd Wright: Ausgeführte Bauten* was richly illustrated with photographs of completed structures and a few plans. Although published in German, Wasmuth provided the English text of C. R. Ashbee's introduction for the foreign market.

11. The printed list of plates includes only sixty-four plates. The eight additional plates are marked in the Roman numeral sequence annotated as "a" or "b."

12. Anthony Alofsin, *Frank Lloyd Wright—The Lost Years, 1910– 1922: A Study of Influence* (Chicago, 1993), p. 77. Alofsin offers one of the most comprehensive histories of the Wasmuth publications. H. Allen Brooks addressed the complex attributions of Wasmuth drawings to the various renderers and architects working for Wright in "Frank Lloyd Wright and the Wasmuth Drawings," *Art Bulletin* 48, 2 (June 1966), pp. 193–202.

13. The Centre Canadien d'Architecture, Montreal, has an advertising brochure published by Wright. He offered the two-portfolio set to "young Architects, draftsmen and students" for $32.00 including the delivery cost, with an approval-plan option and an installment-payment option.

14. The Ryerson and Burnham Libraries possess a number of editions of this work: the original seven special issues; the 1925 edition of the compiled issues entitled *The Life-Work of the American Architect Frank Lloyd Wright,* which was also released by *Wendingen;* the 1948 reissue from A. Kroch and Son, Chicago; and the 1965 edition published by Horizon Press, New York.

15. A succinct history of *Wendingen* was published in Giovanni Fanelli and Ezio Godoli, "Wendingen," *FMR* (English ed.), no. 36 (Jan.-Feb. 1989), pp. 81–96. A more detailed discussion of the publication's history is contained in *Wendingen, 1918–1931: Amsterdamer*

Expressionismus: Ein Architekturmagazin der 20er Jahre vom Stadtebau zur Schriftgestaltung, exh. cat. (Darmstadt, 1992).

16. *The Life-Work of the American Architect Frank Lloyd Wright* (New York, 1965), n. pag.

17. Marion Mahony Griffin donated a second incomplete copy to the Art Institute and another copy to the New-York Historical Society. The present author has not collated the Chicago and New York versions.

18. *Illinois Society of Architects Bulletin* 25, 2–3 (Aug.-Sept. 1940), p. 2.

19. Marion Mahony Griffin, "The Magic of America" (unpub. ms.), section 1, p. 5 (as numbered in upper right corner), Ryerson and Burnham Libraries, The Art Institute of Chicago.

20. For a more comprehensive discussion of the New-York Historical Society version of "The Magic of America," see James Weirick, "'The Magic of America': Vision and Text," in *Walter Burley Griffin: A Re-view* (Clayton, Victoria, Australia, 1988), pp. 5–14.

21. Griffin (note 19), section 2, p. 47 (as numbered in lower right corner).

22. Ibid., section 4, p. 159 (as numbered in lower right corner).

23. Speech by David Gebhard at the annual conference of the Society of Architectural Historians, Seattle, Apr. 1995.

24. Maher was an active member on the committee of the Illinois chapter of the American Institute of Architects, which successfully lobbied the national convention in 1918 to change the organization's regulations. The new regulations permitted an architect's name to be included in signage on a building under construction and on the completed structure. See "The Institute's Attitude on Advertising," *Western Architect* 27, 5 (May 1918), pp. 42–44. Another mechanism that an architect could use to promote his work was product literature such as the book *Representative Cement Houses* (Chicago, 1910), published by the Universal Portland Cement Company, which featured three Maher projects: the Henry Schultz, Emil Rudolph, and Mrs. C. K. Parmelee residences, which were published with physical descriptions, costs, and testimonials by the clients praising the design and the choice of cement as a building material.

25. George W. Maher, "The Western Spirit," *Western Architect* 9, 11 (Nov. 1906), p. 113.

26. American School of Correspondence, "Preface," *Modern American Homes* (Chicago, 1912), n. pag.

27. Related titles published at this time include *Cyclopedia of Architecture, Carpentry and Building: A General Reference Work . . . Prepared by a Staff of Architects, Builders, and Experts of the Highest Professional Standing, Illustrated with over Three Thousand Engravings* (Chicago, 1907–09), and *Building Superintendence: A Working Guide to the Requirements of Modern American Building Practice and the Systematic Supervision of Building Operations* (Chicago, 1910).

28. Upon Wright's return from Europe, the two men disputed the division of architects' fees and design responsibility for continuing and new clients, finally resolving their disagreement in the summer of 1911. See David T. Van Zanten, "The Early Work of Marion Mahony Griffin," *Prairie School Review* 3, 2 (1966), pp. 5–23; and Alofsin (note 12), pp. 68–69, 316–17.

29. For a succinct history of the late nineteenth-century development of architectural terracotta, see Margaret Henderson Floyd, "Architectural Terra Cotta to 1900," *Studio Potter* 17, 1 (Dec. 1988), pp. 32–39.

30. A list of Chicago buildings with their specific uses of terracotta is included in "A Partial List of Buildings in the Chicago Central Area with Terra Cotta Cladding," in Nancy D. Berryman and Susan M. Tindall, *Terra Cotta: Preservation of an Historic Building Material* (Chicago, 1984).

31. For details of Sullivan's stylistic development, see Floyd (note 29), pp. 32–39; and Wim de Wit, ed., *Louis Sullivan: The Function of Ornament,* exh. cat. (Chicago, 1986).

32. For more information on the Chicago firms, see Sharon S. Darling, *Architectural Terra Cotta in Chicago* (New York, 1992); and idem, *Chicago Ceramics and Glass: An Illustrated History from 1871 to 1933,* exh. cat. (Chicago, 1979).

33. From 1907 to 1940, Alschuler designed nearly 125 buildings using products from the American Terra Cotta and Ceramic Company, which are listed in Statler Gilfillen, ed., *The American Terra Cotta Index* (Palos Park, Ill., 1972), p. 191.

34. See discussion of Alschuler's low-rise commercial architecture in C. W. Westfall, "Buildings Serving Commerce," in John Zukowsky, ed., *Chicago Architecture, 1872–1922: Birth of a Metropolis,* exh. cat. (Chicago, 1987), pp. 76–89.

35. *Beauty and Utility in Concrete* (Chicago, 1914), p. 5.

36. Numerous publications praised concrete's appropriateness for residences around this time: *Concrete Houses and Cottages* (published in two volumes by the Atlas Portland Cement Company in 1909); *The Concrete House and Its Construction* (Association of American Portland Cement Manufacturers, 1912); *Representative Cement Houses* (Universal Portland Cement Company, c. 1910); and William A. Radford's *Cement Houses and How to Build Them* (Radford Architectural Company, c. 1909).

37. The production history of Teco wares has been discussed in

detail in Sharon S. Darling, *Teco: Art Pottery of the Prairie School*, exh. cat. (Erie, Pa., 1989); and Darling, *Chicago Ceramics and Glass* (note 32).

38. Gates Potteries, *Hints for Gifts and Home Decoration* (Chicago, 1905), p. 7.

39. Thomas Eddy Tallmadge, "The 'Chicago School,'" *Architectural Review* 15, 4 (Apr. 1908), p. 73; quoted in Darling, *Chicago Ceramics and Glass* (note 32), p. 59.

40. For a general history of the Kalo Shop, see Sharon S. Darling and Gail Farr Casterline, *Chicago Metalsmiths: An Illustrated History*, exh. cat. (Chicago, 1977).

41. Excerpt from lecture by William Morris, published in Aymer Vallance, *William Morris: His Art, His Writings, and His Public Life* (London, 1898), p. 438.

42. Wright designed a residence in Buffalo, New York, for Hubbard's brother-in-law, William R. Heath. Wright and Hubbard probably met during Wright's various trips to Buffalo while working on the Heath and Darwin D. Martin residences and the Larkin Building. John Lloyd Wright provided a tantalizingly brief description of the two personalities: "Elbert Hubbard was almost as picturesque as was Father—they talked arts, crafts and philosophy by the hour. Said Elbert the Hubbard to the Papa one night, 'Modesty being egotism turned wrong side out, let me say here that I am an orator, a great orator! I have health, gesture, imagination, voice, vocabulary, taste, ideas—I acknowledge it myself. What I lack in shape I make up in nerve . . .' Said Dad the Papa to the Hubbard, 'Not only do I intend to be the greatest architect who has yet lived, but the greatest who will ever live . . .' Just a couple of boys trying to get along" (Wright, *My Father Who Is on Earth* [New York, 1946], pp. 32–33).

43. Upon returning to Buffalo, he joined Harry Taber and his Roycroft Printing Shop (the name was taken from the seventeenth-century English bookbinding partners Samuel and Thomas Roycroft), which published the first issue of the "little" magazine *The Philistine: A Periodical of Protest* in June 1895.

44. The Roycroft Press intentionally emulated the style of Morris's Kelmscott Press publications. As one scholar wrote, "Roycroft books consisted of handmade materials, even those composed and printed mechanically; they were bound in leather or paper boards, not cloth; they emphasized decoration, with the use of color, with fleurons, and with ornamented title pages, initials, and colophons; they were usually in an old-style typeface; and the text page layout usually had wide margins and the running title in the form of a shoulder note" (Susan Otis Thompson, *American Book Design and William Morris* [New York, 1977], p. 181).

45. Hubbard employed artists such as William W. Denslow (from 1896 to 1900), who was later well known for his illustrations for Frank Baum's *The Wonderful Wizard of Oz*; and Dard Hunter (employed from 1903 to 1910), who unified the art and craft of the book by making the paper, designing and casting type, and printing the books themselves. The most comprehensive survey of the Roycroft Press is Paul McKenna, *A History and Bibliography of the Roycroft Printing Shop* (North Tonawanda, N.Y., 1986).

46. Gustav Stickley, "Foreword," *Craftsman* 1, 1 (Oct. 1901), p. i. The name United Crafts was changed to Craftsman Workshops around 1904, when Stickley disbanded the guildlike craft community in favor of a more traditional production system.

47. "The Living Room, Its Many Uses and Its Possibilities for Comfort and Beauty," *Craftsman* 9, 1 (Oct. 1905), p. 59.

48. "Als Ik Kan," *Craftsman* 11, 1 (Oct. 1906), p. 128.

49. Stickley adapted Sullivan's essay, which originally appeared in *American Contractor* (Jan. 1906), publishing it in *The Craftsman* in three parts in the May, June, and July issues of 1906.

50. Robert C. Twombly, ed., *Louis Sullivan: The Public Papers* (Chicago, 1988), p. 174.

51. Louis Sullivan, "What Is Architecture? A Study of the American People of Today," *Craftsman* 10, 3 (June 1906), p. 357; reprinted in Twombly, ed. (note 50), p. 188.

52. Sullivan (note 51), p. 356; reprinted in Twombly, ed. (note 50), p. 186.

53. Among the important titles republished by the Prairie School Press are: Marianna Griswold van Rensselaer's *Henry Hobson Richardson and His Works* (1967); Harriet Monroe's biography *John Wellborn Root: A Study of His Life and Work* (1966); and *Architectural Essays from the Chicago School: Thomas Tallmadge, Louis H. Sullivan, Jens Jensen, and Frank Lloyd Wright from 1900 to 1909*, a collection of essays reprinted from *The Architectural Review, The Brickbuilder,* and *Ladies Home Journal,* published in 1967 and edited by Wilbert R. Hasbrouck. The press also published *Wright's Ausgefürte Bauten und Entwürfe von Frank Lloyd Wright* in a smaller format entitled *Studies and Executed Buildings by Frank Lloyd Wright,* with the English translation of Wright's introductory essay originally published by Ralph Fletcher Seymour.

THURMAN, "'Make Designs to Your Heart's Content' The Frank Lloyd Wright/Schumacher Venture," pp. 152–63.

1. In addition to the folio in the Art Institute's collection, copies can be found in: the Cooper-Hewitt National Museum of Design, Smithsonian Institution, New York (one); the Milwaukee Public Library (one); the Frank Lloyd Wright Foundation, Scottsdale, Arizona (hereafter referred to as FLW Foundation) (one); F. Schumacher and Company, New York (five); and private collections in Milwaukee (one) and Hollywood, Calif. (one). At FLW Foundation, the author would like to thank Penny Fowler (Administrator of the Fine Arts Collection for the Frank Lloyd Wright Archives), John deKoven Hill (Honorary Chairman of the Board of Trustees), Bruce Brooks Pfeiffer (Director of Archives), and Ling Po (Fellow), all of whom were generous with their time and knowledge. She is also deeply grateful to René Carrillo and Richard E. Slavin III (Archivist/Historian, F. Schumacher and Company) for their invaluable help with the preparation of this article. All citations from Frank Lloyd Wright are © The Frank Lloyd Wright Foundation, 1995.

2. A contract in the form of a letter from Wright to F. Schumacher and Company was signed on Mar. 11, 1954 (microfiche of archival materials in FLW Foundation, J. Paul Getty Museum, Malibu, Calif. [hereafter referred to as Getty microfiche]); Wright saw the first samples in August of that year; and the entire line was ready for its inaugural display in model rooms by fall 1955. In addition to correspondence in the Getty microfiche and FLW Foundation, valuable documentation has been provided in an unpublished manuscript by René Carrillo, "Recollections of Frank Lloyd Wright" (1988), which he kindly made available to the author.

3. House Beautiful 98, 11 (Nov. 1955). The issue was entitled "Frank Lloyd Wright: His Contribution to the Beauty of American Life."

4. Letter from Charles Fabens Kelley, Assistant Director, to Daniel Catton Rich, Director, The Art Institute of Chicago, July 21, 1953; and letter from Kelley to Wright, Sept. 3, 1953, both in the The Art Institute of Chicago Archives (hereafter referred to as AIC Archives); "Taliesin Students to Offer Dances, Rituals" and "Taliesin Dancers to Perform," in Chicago Sunday Tribune, Nov. 1, 1953 (AIC Archives); and playbill dated Nov. 3, 1953 (FLW Foundation). The museum's administration was somewhat hesitant about allowing such an event to take place on its premises, but was persuaded by Wright himself, who came to the museum accompanied by his daughter Iovanna. Wright said that, if pressed, he himself would provide a brief introduction to the various elements of the evening. Judging from the press coverage the event attracted (see above), he apparently agreed to speak at the performance. Wright paid $250 for the use of the theater, and the public paid $1.50 per ticket. The costumes used were designed and painted at Taliesin; a leading member of the design team was Ling

Po (communication from Bruce Brooks Pfeiffer to the Department of Textiles, The Art Institute of Chicago, Nov. 21, 1988).

5. On Wright's interest in machine technology, see Frank Lloyd Wright, "The Art and Craft of the Machine," lecture delivered at Hull House, Chicago, Mar. 1, 1901, in Bruce Brooks Pfeiffer, ed., Frank Lloyd Wright: Collected Writings, vol. 1 (New York, 1992), pp. 58–69. In a late essay (1958), Wright extolled the virtues of modern technology to reproduce and standardize the work of the architect, with the proviso that principles of good design must be followed; see "Prefabrication," in ibid., vol. 5 (New York, 1995), pp. 234–38. Wright provided designs for the Dutch Leerdam Glass Company in 1930; one vase was executed but apparently never manufactured; see David A. Hanks, The Decorative Designs of Frank Lloyd Wright (New York, 1979), pp. 185–86, and p. 187, fig. 200.

6. Interview by author with John deKoven Hill, Jan. 6, 1988; and Carrillo (note 2), p. 4. Perhaps Wright was unaware that for years his associates had procured fabrics from F. Schumacher and Company: "mohair," "satin," and "taffeta" were ordered for some of Wright's early, classic Prairie School houses. These included the Avery Coonley House (1907; Riverside, Ill.) and the Frederick Robie House (1906–09; Chicago); see Hanks (note 5), p. 219.

7. Carrillo (note 2), p. 5.

8. Ibid.

9. On F. Schumacher and Company, see Richard E. Slavin III, Opulent Textiles: The Schumacher Collection (New York, 1992); Christa C. Mayer Thurman, "F. Schumacher & Company," in Montreal, Musée des Arts Décoratifs, Design 1935–1965: What Modern Was, exh. cat., ed. Martin Eidelberg (New York, 1991), p. 373; and Hanks (note 5), pp. 217–19.

10. Slavin, "A Century in the Trade," memo to Schumacher Centennial Committee dated Aug. 27, 1986, p. 4 (copy in the files of the Department of Textiles, The Art Institute of Chicago; hereafter referred to as AIC Textile files).

11. Letter from Carrillo to Wright, Mar. 22, 1954 (Getty microfiche).

12. Vincent Scully, "Foreword," in Hanks (note 5), pp. iii-iv.

13. Linen napkins designed for the Coonley House are illustrated in Hanks (note 5), p. 105, fig. 105. On Wright's dress designs, see John Lloyd Wright, My Father Who Is on Earth (New York, 1946), pp. 41–42; and Hanks (note 5), pp. 24–26.

14. For the illustration of the Dana House textile, see IC Corporation and The Art Institute of Chicago, Frank Lloyd Wright—The Early Years: The 1910 Frank Lloyd Wright Wasmuth Portfolio Calendar (Palos Park, Ill., 1975), pl. 21b. On the Imperial Hotel, see Bruce Brooks Pfeiffer, ed., Frank Lloyd Wright Preliminary Studies, 1889–1916, photographs by Yukio Futagawa (Tokyo,

1985), vol. 9, p. 144. For a color illustration of one of the Bogk House carpets, see Hanks (note 5), pl. 11.

15. See Wright, Taliesin Fellowship lecture, Mar. 7, 1954, p. 4, reel 93a (FLW Foundation), © FLW Foundation. In addition to those in the FLW Foundation, designs for the Bogk House carpets can be found in the Centre Canadien d'Architecture, Montreal, and in several private collections. The chart with actual yarn samples, which was provided to the manufacturer, is in the Prairie Archives of the Milwaukee Art Museum.

16. For an illustration of the sketch for the original curtain, see Hanks (note 5), p. 144, fig. 159.

17. On Wright's displeasure with interior designers, see Wright, Taliesin Fellowship lecture, Aug. 22, 1954, p. 7, reel 104 (FLW Foundation), © FLW Foundation; and Carrillo (note 2), p. 11. On Marion Mahony's involvement with interior accessory design, see H. Allen Brooks, *The Prairie School: Frank Lloyd Wright and His Midwest Contemporaries* (Toronto, 1972), p. 79. The Prairie Archives at the Milwaukee Art Museum contain numerous documents and references attesting to Niedecken's selection and ordering of textiles for Wright projects.

In 1937 Wright also collaborated with the textile artist Loja Saarinen, wife of architect Eliel; see The Detroit Institute of Arts and The Metropolitan Museum of Art, New York, *Design in America: The Cranbrook Vision, 1925–1950,* exh. cat. by Robert Judson Clark et al. (New York, 1983), p. 189, and p. 318 n. 80. For his interiors, he also used the fabrics of famed textile designer Dorothy Liebes; some of these appear in photographs of Wright's interiors included in the issue of *House Beautiful* devoted to him ([note 3], pp. 261, 338, and 371).

18. Letter from Carrillo to the author, July 17, 1995, AIC Textile files.

19. See Carrillo (note 11).

20. Wright (note 15), p. 6.

21. Carrillo (note 2), p. 7.

22. Ibid., p. 9.

23. On the nature of Po's involvement with the Schumacher project, see letter from Penny Fowler to the author, Mar. 22, 1989, AIC Textile files. Po has also helped clarify the relationship to the venture of eight large designs presented by René Carrillo to the Archives of American Art, which has since become part of the Smithsonian Institute, Washington, D.C. From Sept. 2 to Oct. 31, 1988, three of them were included in an exhibition at the Elvehjem Museum, Madison, Wisconsin. This exhibition, called "The House Beautiful: Frank Lloyd Wright For Everyone," focused on the November 1955 *House Beautiful* issue. It was held concurrently with a larger display, entitled "Frank Lloyd Wright in Madison: Eight Decades of Artistic and Social Interaction." The three works were mistakenly labeled as designs for carpets. The Archives of American Art had been identifying them as wallpaper designs. In fact, Po, who was responsible for all eight designs, and Bruce Brooks Pfeiffer have indicated that, while they were inspired by the Coonley House carpets, they were in fact intended as curtain material. They were initially intended to be part of the Wright/Schumacher venture, but the company ultimately rejected them. According to Po, Schumacher then supplied its own designs, which Wright "edited and corrected prior to [their] going into production." See letter from Pfeiffer to author, Nov. 21, 1988, AIC Textile files.

24. Terracotta red must have been a very special color for Wright, since not only did it pervade and accent his graphic designs, but at least at one point, as Carrillo noted, all of the architect's cars were painted that color; see Carrillo (note 2), p. 7. On Wright's love of expensive cars, see Jim Hockenhull, "Trekking to Usonia: Frank Lloyd Wright's Crosley Cars," *Frank Lloyd Wright Quarterly* 3, 1 (Winter, 1992), pp. 4–8. According to Carrillo, the textiles were printed in part by Printex, Ossining, N.Y. (the company of Vera Newman, who became famous for her scarves) and the New Jersey-based firm Old Deerfield, which also printed the wallpapers (telephone communication with the author, Mar. 14, 1989).

25. "And now Frank Lloyd Wright designs home furnishings you can buy," in *House Beautiful* (note 3), p. 285. The same caption states that design 104 is "typical of how Mr. Wright achieves ornament from 'geometric gaiety.'"

26. See Pfeiffer (note 23) and Wright (note 2), which lists "fabrics, carpets, wallpapers."

27. David A. Hanks, *The Decorative Designs of Frank Lloyd Wright,* exh. cat. (New York, 1978). An advertisement for Karastan in the *House Beautiful* issue dedicated to Wright (note 3) features the words "On the Way" and states, "The Taliesin Collection, to be introduced next Spring, is still on the drawing boards. But we can safely predict that it will be as beautiful and liveable, as thoughtful and original as everything this great designer has done" (p. 349).

28. *House Beautiful* (note 3), p. 282.

29. Interview with John deKoven Hill (note 6); letter to Wright from T. Henry Wilson (FLW Foundation).

30. Letter from Wright to Edwards, Nov. 24, 1956 (FLW Foundation).

31. Carrillo (note 2), p. 10.

32. Ibid., p. 11.

33. Undated letter from Wright to Carrillo (Getty microfiche). That the opening was scheduled for Oct. 17, 1955, is indicated in a telegram, dated Aug. 23, from Carrillo inviting Wright to the event (Getty microfiche).

34. Letter from Carrillo to Wright, Sept. 9, 1955 (Getty microfiche).

35. "And now Frank Lloyd Wright designs . . ." (note 25), pp. 282–90, 336–39.

36. Carrillo (note 2), p. 19. Wright wrote two letters to Carrillo during this period, dated Oct. 6 and 19, 1955; Carrillo wrote once to Wright, on Oct. 13 (Getty microfiche).

37. See letters from Carrillo to Wright from 1956: Jan. 19, July 3, Oct. 11, and Dec. 12 (Getty microfiche).

38. Letter from Carrillo to Wright, Nov. 12, 1956 (Getty microfiche).

39. On the Schumacher products introduced in 1986, see F. Schumacher and Company brochure for fall 1986 (a copy is in AIC Textile files). The company's archives contain price lists and correspondence relating to the line after 1955. Interestingly, these new designs, gathered under the rubric "Frank Lloyd Wright," include a group entitled "Imperial." They were inspired by Wright's textile designs for the Imperial Hotel, Tokyo. On Oct. 6, 1955, Wright wrote Carrillo (note 36) that he was sending, from his vault, some textile samples from the hotel project, because he thought they might be of interest to Schumacher. Carrillo replied on Oct. 19 (note 36) that they would indeed stimulate further designs. This indeed happened, over thirty years later!

PREGLIASCO, "The Life and Work of Marion Mahony Griffin," pp. 164–81.

1. *1894 Class Book, Massachusetts Institute of Technology* (Cambridge, Mass., 1898).

2. Barry Byrne, "The Chicago Movement" (unpub. ms., 1939), Ricker Architectural Library, University of Illinois at Champaign-Urbana.

3. Letter from John Lloyd Wright to Mark Peisch, Jan. 22, 1969, Avery Architectural Library, Columbia University, New York (referred to hereafter as AAL).

4. Richard W. Bock, "The Autobiography of Richard W. Bock" (unpub. ms., 1946), chap. 10, p. 9.

5. Susan Fondiler Berkon and Jane Holtz Kay, "Marion Mahony Griffin, Architect," *Feminist Art Journal* 4, 1 (Spring 1975), pp. 10–14.

6. David Van Zanten, "The Early Work of Marion Mahony Griffin," *Prairie School Review* 3, 2 (1966), p. 10.

7. Marion Mahony Griffin, "Democratic Architecture, Part I," *Building* (Sydney) (June 12, 1914), p. 102.

8. Letter from Marion Mahony Griffin to William Gray Purcell, Aug. 7, 1947, William Gray Purcell Papers, Correspondence, Northwest Architectural Archives, University of Minnesota Libraries, St. Paul.

9. Maya Moran, the owner of Wright's Tomek House (1907; Riverside, Ill.), has described the various feelings brought by diurnal changes: "Throw open all those windows and the entire feeling changes. Suddenly one is in a fishbowl and one realizes the art glass creates the privacy in a house with more windows than walls. . . . The outside becomes an extension of the inside in the daytime, not just because the casement windows swing out, but because of the colorations of the art glass. At night the iridescence is on the inside and the windows are not black holes but sparkling jewels. It is also at night that . . . the unusual fenestration seems to articulate more clearly the horizontality of the house." See Moran, "Looking through Wright Windows," *Professional Stained Glass* (May 1991), p. 16.

10. Letter from Barry Byrne to Mark Peisch, Mar. 22, 1960, AAL. Mahony and Wright's collaborative design process during the early years of the decade is illustrated by Byrne's description in the same letter: "[In 1903] Marion . . . was occupied in designing glass and furniture under Wright's direction. In justice to her, I must add that Wright's 'directions' often consisted only of his approval. It is also to be noted that the 'style' of these articles followed that which Wright had initiated." Marion's independent art glass designs are the closest to Wright's in composition, color, design, and delicacy.

11. Drawings for the glass designs are dated as late as November 1909, two months after Wright's departure from North America. None of the previous elevation drawings for the home indicated window panes or patterns, and no perspective drawings of the house had been done. The project was one of the Wright's "in progress" projects to be completed by Marion's staff in the von Holst office.

12. According to Roy Lippincott, "In these three houses we did everything including the design of furniture, carpets, draperies, silver services and linens. They were all exclusively Marion's design" (letter from Lippincott to Mark Peisch, Nov. 28, 1954, AAL).

13. Eileen Michels, "The Early Drawings of Frank Lloyd Wright Reconsidered," *Journal of the Society of Architectural Historians* 30, 4 (Dec. 1971), pp. 294–303.

14. Barry Byrne, review of *The Drawings of Frank Lloyd Wright*, by Arthur Drexler, *Journal of the Society of Architectural Historians* 12, 2 (May 1963), pp. 108–09.

15. Vincent Scully, *Studies and Executed Buildings by Frank Lloyd Wright* (New York, 1986), p. 5.

16. H. Allen Brooks, Jr., "Frank Lloyd Wright and the Wasmuth Drawings," *Art Bulletin* 48, 2 (June 1966), p. 20.

17. Grant Carpenter Manson, *Frank Lloyd Wright to 1910: The First Golden Age* (New York, 1958), app. f; Robert C. Twombly, *Frank Lloyd Wright: An Interpretive Biography* (New York, 1973), p. 171; and Barry Byrne, conversation with Mark Peisch, Apr. 25, 1953, AAL.

18. Marion Mahony Griffin, "The Magic of America" (unpub. ms.), Ryerson and Burnham Libraries, The Art Institute of Chicago.

19. Grant Carpenter Manson, "Notes for *Frank Lloyd Wright to 1910: The First Golden Age:* January 1940 Interview with Marion Mahony Griffin" (unpub. ms.), Grant Carpenter Manson Papers, Oak Park Public Library, Oak Park, Ill.

20. Griffin, "The Magic of America" (note 18), vol. 4 ("The Individual Battle").

21. Letter from Barry Byrne to Mark Peisch, Jan. 21, 1969, AAL.

22. See, for example, H. Allen Brooks, *The Prairie School: Frank Lloyd Wright and His Midwest Contemporaries* (Toronto, 1972), p. 165.

23. Letter from Roy Lippincott to Mark Peisch, Nov. 28, 1954, AAL.

24. Letter from Barry Byrne to Mark Peisch, Mar. 29, 1965, AAL.

25. Van Zanten (note 6), p. 22.

26. See Jaqueline Robertson, "A Fresh Look at the Future of a Capital Idea," *Inland Architect* 25, 1 (Jan./Feb. 1981), pp. 7–11. Robertson's article is a clear analysis of Walter's plan for Canberra and a compelling argument for its realization.

27. Editorial, "The Federal Capital for the Commonwealth of Australia," *Town Planning Review* (London) 3, 3 (Oct. 1912), pp. 165–67.

28. A plaque in the refectory commemorates Marion's design of the space.

29. Roy Lippincott said, "He [Griffin] did little actual drafting at this time" (letter from Lippincott to Mark Peisch, Nov. 28, 1954, AAL). Griffin employees of the period also reported never having seen him at a drawing table.

30. Statement by Marion Mahony Griffin to family members, reported by both Larry Perkins and Jean Hayes Beard.

31. Marion Mahony Griffin, "The Magic of America" (note 18), vol. 1 ("The Empirial Battle"). Marion was at the drawing board hours after her arrival in Lucknow. The self-described "slave of the drafting room" spent twelve hours a day, six to seven days a week, for the next several months designing as well as supervising an Indian drafting force. As in Australia, Walter represented the office to the outside world, and he was involved in the numerous introductory meetings required by Indian clients as well as contractors and governmental officials.

32. Charles E. White, Jr., "Letters from the Studio of F. L. Wright (1903–1906)," *Journal of Architectural Education* 25 (Fall 1971), p. 110.

33. Letter from Roy Lippincott to Mark Peisch, Nov. 28, 1954, AAL.

34. Reyner Banham, "Death and Life of the Prairie School," *Architectural Review* 154 (Aug. 1973), p. 101.

EDITOR'S ACKNOWLEDGMENTS

I wish to thank the Graham Foundation for Advanced Studies in the Fine Arts for its financial support of this issue of *Museum Studies.* I am grateful to Anthony Alofsin, John Eifler, David A. Hanks, Cheryl Robertson, and Pauline Saliga for their early and enthusiastic help with this project. I must also thank the following staff members of the Art Institute for all of their hard work in raising funds for this issue: Greg Cameron, Director of Exhibition and Special Project Funding; Karin Victoria, Director of Government Relations; and Greg Perry, Associate Director of Government Relations.

I would like to thank the authors of this issue for their outstanding contributions and their unfailing congeniality. I also wish to thank the following staff members of the Art Institute for their work on this issue: Susan F. Rossen, Executive Director of Publications, and Robert V. Sharp, Associate Director of Publications, for their considerable help in editing the manuscripts; Ann Wassmann, Associate Director of Graphic Design and Communication Services, for her superb design of this issue; Jack Brown, Executive Director of the Ryerson and Burnham Libraries, for his insightful comments on the manuscripts; John Zukowsky, Curator of Architecture, for his words of advice and encouragement; Bryan Miller, Cris Ligenza, and Britt Salvesen of the Publications Department for performing many indispensable tasks; Bob Hashimoto, Greg Williams, Annie Morse, and Pam Stuedemann of the Department of Imaging and Technical Services for their dedicated efforts on our behalf; and Annemarie van Roessel of the Department of Architecture for reading galleys and tracking down hard-to-find facts. Finally, I must express my deep gratitude to Manine Golden, who has worked on the production of *Museum Studies* for the last three years. Everyone in the Publications Department at the Art Institute wishes her the greatest success in her new job at Marquand Books in Seattle.